INSIGHT COMPACT GUIDE

Compact Guide: Boston is the ultimate quick-reference guide to this fascinating destination. It tells you all you need to know about Boston's attractions, from Beacon Hill to Back Bay and from Quincy Market to Harvard Square, not forgetting its legendary museums and historic nearby towns.

This is one of 130 Compact Guides, combining the interests and enthusiasms of two of the world's best known information providers: Insight Guides, whose titles have set the standard for visual travel guides since 1970, and Discovery Channel, the world's premier source of non-fiction television programming.

APA PUBLICATIONS

Part of the Langenscheidt Publishing Group

Insight Compact Guide: Boston

Written by Christopher Kennedy
Updated by Natasha Babaian
Main photography: Mark Read
Additional photography: Essex Institute, Salem (8), Museum of Fine Arts
(9/2), Catherine Karnow (90), Ken Mallory (91, 93), Roger Williams (88)
Cover picture: Mark Read
Edited by: Siân Lezard
Design: Roger Williams
Picture Editor: Hilary Genin
Maps: Polyglott/Buchhaupt

Editorial Director: Brian Bell
Managing Editor: Tony Halliday

CONTACTING THE EDITORS: As every effort is made to provide accurate
information in this publication, we would appreciate it if readers would
call our attention to any errors and omissions by contacting:
Apa Publications, PO Box 7910, London SE1 1WE, England.
Fax: (44 20) 7403 0290
e-mail: insight@apaguide.demon.co.uk

Information has been obtained from sources believed to be reliable,
but its accuracy and completeness, and the opinions based thereon,
are not guaranteed.

© 2002 APA Publications GmbH & Co. Verlag KG Singapore Branch, Singapore.

First Edition 1997. Second Edition 2002.
Printed in Singapore by Insight Print Services (Pte) Ltd
Original edition © Polyglott-Verlag Dr Bolte KG, Munich

Distributed in the United States by:
Langenscheidt Publishers, Inc.
46–35 54th Road, Maspeth, NY 11378
Tel: (1 718) 784-0055, fax: (1 718) 784-0640

Distributed in the UK & Ireland by:
GeoCenter International Ltd
The Viables Centre, Harrow Way, Basingstoke,
Hampshire RG22 4BJ
Tel: (44 1256) 817987, fax: (44 1256) 817-988

Worldwide distribution enquiries:
APA Publications GmbH & Co. Verlag KG (Singapore Branch)
38 Joo Koon Road, Singapore 628990
Tel: (65) 6865-1600, fax: (65) 6861-6438

www.insightguides.com

BOSTON

Introduction

Places

Culture

Travel Tips

▽ **State House (p22)**
One of the finest buildings in the US, the State House was completed in 1798.

◁ **John Harvard (p67)** He didn't actually found the famous college but his legacy helped fund its early expansion.

▷ **Isabelle Stewart Gardner Museum (p62)** An eclectic range of art, including many master-pieces, is housed here.

◁ **Public Garden (p55)** These 'swan boats' are a well known feature of this park, the oldest botanical garden in the US; it dates from 1839 and is planted with thousands of flowers.

▷ **Concord (p77)** Every year on Patriots' Day the start of the American Revolution is re-enacted in Concord.

◁ **Faneuil Hall (p27)** First built as a market place in 1742, this is the hub of Boston, with shops and restaurants galore.

△ **USS Constitution (p37)** Launched in 1797, this ship fought in many battles; navy seamen now give guided tours.

▷ **Rocky Neck Art Colony (p87)** Galleries and art studios enliven this charming spot.

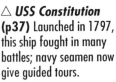

◁ **Battle Road (p77)** The road along which the British marched to Concord in April 1775, triggering events which led to the American Revolution.

▷ **Salem (p81)** The place most closely linked with witchcraft, after 19 alleged witches were hanged here in 1692.

America's 'European' City

Inevitably, visitors to Boston will hear the city and its environs called many things: 'the Athens of America,' 'the hub of the universe' and the 'home of the bean and the cod.' These well-worn sobriquets still have a ring of truth, though most are based on legend. Few Bostonians would now argue that theirs is the nation's cultural or intellectual center as it was a century ago. New York City has seized the title and will not relinquish it. As for the bean and the cod, they may still be found, if only on souvenirs.

Contemporary Boston is America's 'European' city. It is so because of many things: its compact size and pedestrian-friendly streets; three centuries of architectural heritage; sidewalk cafés and cultural institutions. Moreover, Boston is an American city where tradition matters – a rarity in a nation that worships the new.

THE SETTLERS

John Winthrop, aboard the *Arbella* en route from England to the New World in 1630, turned to his fellow Puritans and said, 'We must consider that we shall be as a City upon a Hill. The eyes of all people are upon us.' Winthrop either had remarkable foresight, or he had consulted Capt John Smith who, in 1614, had made a detailed survey of the Massachusetts Bay region.

On reaching the New World, the colonists first landed at Salem, 20 miles (32km) north of Boston but, finding the town in a 'sad and unexpected condition,' they soon moved south to Charlestown. Here, foul drinking water felled the settlers at an alarming rate. When they were visited by the Rev. William Blackstone, who invited them to his home on what is now Boston's Beacon Hill (then called Shawmut), they decided to stay put.

Soon afterward, in honor of the small town in Lincolnshire, England, from which many of the settlers had come,

> ### The Boston mind
> 'Only Bostonians can understand Bostonians and thoroughly sympathise with the inconsequences of the Boston mind'
> – *The Education of Henry Adams* (1907).

Left: Acorn Street, Beacon Hill
Below: reviving the past

Trimountain became Boston. The settlement, whose charter from James I designated it the Massachusetts Bay Company, enjoyed virtual autonomy from the mother country for almost 50 years. It developed as a society in which religion and government were inseparable. Education strictly enforced the moral code. Boston Public Latin School, opened in 1635, was the first free public school and the first secondary school in America. A year later, Harvard, named after its benefactor, opened as a college for ministers.

HANGING WITCHES

Morality over-reached itself in 1648 when the Rev. Cotton Mather 'discovered' that Boston was infested with witches, and subsequently hung three Salem women. It was not until 1693 that Governor Phips put an end to that madness. Boston prospered, not from the land, which was poor for farming, but from the sea – cod fishing, whaling, shipbuilding, and a maritime trade made possible by the excellent natural harbor.

By the 1640s Boston ships were carrying dried cod to feed the African slaves who worked the British-owned sugar plantations in the West Indies. In exchange Bostonians received sugar and gold and, by the 1670s, they had the lion's share of the West Indian shipping business.

Witchcraft trial in 1692

During the following century, England continued to impose increasingly damaging taxes on the young Boston economy. 'Taxation without representation is tyranny' became a rallying cry, and resulted in nearly 100 settlers dressed up as Indians protesting against the tea tax by hurling 340 crates of tea into the harbor, an event later dubbed the Boston Tea Party. Throughout New England, militia units drilled and built up arms caches. Further confrontation was inevitable.

Below: British troops open fire in King Street, from an engraving by revolutionary hero Paul Revere
Bottom: Paul Revere by John Singleton Copley

THE REVOLUTION

The American Revolution began in and around Boston; it was here, in April 1775, that Paul Revere rode out to warn other Bostonians that British troops were preparing for action *(see page 74)*. His 'midnight ride' and the Battle of Bunker Hill are inscribed in the pages of history. When George Washington, who took command of the Continental Army in July 1775, fortified Dorchester Heights, the bell tolled for the British, who evacuated on March 17, 1776, and peace resulted.

In 1787 Charles Bulfinch returned to Boston after traveling in Europe and, influenced by his trip, launched an architectural renaissance. In the second half of the 19th century, Boston earned its reputation as the most diversified and dynamic center of educational, cultural, and medical-scientific activities in the United States.

THE POPULATION

When the Europeans arrived, the New England coast was inhabited by loosely affiliated Algonquin tribes, including the Massachusetts based in the Boston area. Today, the Brahmins claim to be the true Bostonians. The term was coined by Oliver Wendell Holmes to describe certain individuals, some of whom claimed to trace their ancestry to the Arbella, 'with their houses by Bulfinch, their monopoly of Beacon Street, their ancestral portraits and Chinese porcelain, humanitarianism, Unitarian faith in the march of mind, Yankee shrewdness, and New England exclusiveness.'

Cod save us all

Settlers who arrived in 1630 discovered that while Boston's land proved poor for farming, its waters were rich with cod. By the 1740s, vessels from Boston were supplying large quantities of dried cod to feed African slaves who toiled on sugar plantations in the British West Indies. In fact, its prosperous cod market soon expanded as far afield as the Mediterranean. So grateful to the 'sacred cod' was Boston that in 1784, an image of the codfish was hung in the representatives' chamber of the State House, where it remains to this day.

In the 1840s, a spreading rot blighted the potato crop in Ireland, causing widespread famine and emigration. The Irish poured into Boston and, by 1855, some 55,000 had settled in the city, mainly in the North End. It wasn't long before James Curley, John F Fitzgerald (the legendary 'Honey Fitz'), and the Kennedy clan were busy climbing the political ladder.

Today, half of Boston's 60,000 residents are classified as white, nearly a quarter are black, 10 percent are Hispanic and 10 percent Asian. Minority strongholds and white working-class enclaves – South Boston, the North End, Chinatown – still exist, but their ambience is being eroded by the influx of young urban professionals and subsequent gentrification.

Below: beloved cod
Bottom: summertime chess in Harvard Square

LOCATION

The major port in Massachusetts Bay, Boston covers 105 sq miles (272 sq km); around 3 million people live in Greater Boston, which engulfs 100 towns. Cambridge, separated from Boston by the Charles River, is a city in its own right.

CLIMATE

Boston's weather is nothing if not changeable. Air masses from Canada and the Great Lakes collide

with temperate Gulf Stream currents, and erratic weather patterns are influenced by the multiple air masses operating throughout the region. Fall and spring are magnificent, while summers can be oppressively steamy. Winter winds can rival those of Chicago, and recent years have seen unusually mild winters with light snowfall.

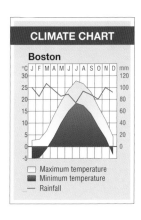

CLIMATE CHART

Boston

Maximum temperature
Minimum temperature
Rainfall

POLITICS

America's great political dynasties – with the exception perhaps of New York's Roosevelts – are Masssachusetts families. Vastly different in many ways, the Adams and Kennedy clans share a remarkable gift for passing through the generations a taste for power. John Adams was the first ambassador to Great Britain, America's first vice-president and its second president. Abigail Adams is remembered today not only as the wife and mother of a president, but as the mother of American feminism; in 1776, she urged her husband to 'Remember the Ladies' at the fateful Continental Congress where independence was declared.

John and Abigail's son, John Quincy Adams, was 26 when Washington appointed him ambassador to the Netherlands; as Secretary of State, Adams *fils* wrote the Monroe Doctrine and succeeded Monroe to the White House. As Lincoln's ambassador to Great Britain, Charles Francis Adams won the struggle to maintain Britain's neutrality in the American Civil War.

The Kennedys' line of public service comes through the Fitzgerald family. John 'Honey Fitz' Fitzgerald, father of Rose, was Boston's first Irish Catholic mayor. John Fitzgerald Kennedy, eldest son of Rose and Joseph Patrick Kennedy, an immensely successful businessman, entered politics at 29 when elected to the US Congress. In 1960, 'JFK' became America's first Catholic president and, at 43, the youngest ever elected. His brother, Edward 'Ted' Kennedy, went to the Senate in 1962 and has been reelected ever since.

'His Honor' James Michael Curley was the city's quintessential politician. Born of poor Irish immigrants and orphaned at an early age, Curley

JF Kennedy statue outside the State House

epitomized the cultural clash of upstart Irish against entrenched Brahmins. He was elected Mayor of Boston four times, including a landslide victory in 1945 while under federal indictment for mail fraud. Later convicted, the 'Mayor of the Poor' insisted he had 'done it for a friend.'

Below: Harvard Yard Science Centre and (bottom) the Carpenter Center, on campus

ECONOMY

The latter years of the 20th century saw a new industrial revolution in Boston. By the 1980s, Boston was the hub of the Massachusetts Miracle, based largely on high tech and venture capital. Even the recession that hit New England in the early 1990s quickly lifted, and the city rebounded, stronger than ever. Route 128, a highway encircling the city, is now lined with so many high-tech firms it's known as America's Technology Highway.

EDUCATION AND SCIENCE

The city remains a center for learning and publishing, and the strong student presence lends a youthful vigor to the city. Boston University, where Martin Luther King studied philosophy and developed the non-violent principles of the civil rights movement, is acclaimed as one of the nation's best city schools, and The Massachusetts

Institute of Technology (MIT), established in 1861, is a leader in its field. Boston hospitals' 'firsts' include the first kidney transplant at Brigham Hospital (1953); the first open heart surgery at Children's Hospital (1967); and development of artificial skin for burn victims (1981).

Bostonians have made lasting contributions in other areas of science. Alexander Graham Bell and his assistant Thomas Watson developed the telephone in a Boston garret in 1876. In 1944, a team of scientists from Harvard, MIT and the US Navy developed the 'Mark I,' a digitally-programmed calculating machine more than 50 feet (15 meters) long, which ushered in the computer age. In Cambridge, Edwin Land's lens manufacturing company introduced the first Polaroid instant 'Land' camera here in 1947.

Sporting highlights
The Sports Museum of New England, located at 1 Fleet Center, pays tribute to New England's athletes and teams through interactive exhibits, memorabilia, art, and video footage. Open Tues–Sat from 10am–5pm, Sun from noon–5pm; hours may change due to events (tel: 624-1234).

SPORTS

As serious as Boston's reputation may seem, the city has provided its share of athletic and sporting diversion. In 1863, the Oneida Football Club was formed by area students as the first such club in the United States, and was never defeated in three years of play on Boston Common. Over time, 'Boston rules' for football – liberally adapted from rugby and soccer – were adopted by American colleges.

In 1903, the Boston Pilgrims (later, the Boston Red Sox) defeated the Pittsburgh Pirates in the first modern World Series. Fenway Park opened in 1912 with a Red Sox victory against the New York Yankees, and the rivalry continues unabated. Hometown hero George Herman 'Babe' Ruth combined remarkable pitching and hitting abilities and sparked the Red Sox's dominance of the majors between 1914 and 1918.

Basketball was invented in Massachusetts at Springfield, and the Boston Celtics have until recently dominated play in the National Basketball Association. In 1995, the Celtics and the Boston Bruins of the National Hockey League moved from the legendary, if aging, Boston Garden to the sleek new FleetCenter.

League lads

HISTORICAL HIGHLIGHTS

1625 William Blackstone, a 29-year-old Anglican clergyman, is Boston's first European settler, building a log cabin on what is now Boston Common.

1630 John Winthrop, governor of the Massachusetts Bay Company, leads Puritan ships into Boston Harbor after a three-month trip from England.

1635 Boston Latin School, the nation's first public school, is founded.

1636 The Puritans found a college at Newetowne, later Cambridge, to be named after its benefactor, John Harvard.

1640 Stephen Day publishes the first book in the colonies, *Bay Psalm Book.*

1660 Quaker Mary Dyer is hanged on Boston Common. Quakers are denounced by Puritans as a 'cursed sect.'

1684 Massachusetts Bay Colony charter is revoked, ending Puritan independence from royal control.

1690 The first American newspaper, *Publick Occurrences: Both Foreign and Domestic*, is published in Boston.

1692 Salem Witch Trials begin.

1717 Boston Light, the oldest lighthouse in the nation, is erected in the harbor.

1764 Sugar Act and Stamp Act arouse anti-royalist sentiments.

1770 Boston Massacre: British troops fire on a rock-throwing mob, killing five.

1773 Boston Tea Party – a shipment of tea is thrown into the harbor in protest against a new three-pence tax on tea. Phillis Wheatley, a young slave living with a wealthy Boston family, is the first published African-American poet.

1775 Paul Revere's ride and Battles of Lexington and Concord spark American Revolution. Battle of Bunker Hill. George Washington takes command of Continental Army at Cambridge.

1776 British troops evacuate Boston. Declaration of Independence read from the Old State House balcony.

1780 John Adams drafts Massachusetts Constitution including a Bill of Rights; John Hancock is first governor of the Commonwealth of Massachusetts.

1795 New State House by Charles Bulfinch, America's first architect.

1812 The War of 1812 against the British paralyzes the city's commerce.

1814 Industrial Revolution begins at Charles River mill.

1815 Handel & Haydn Society, the nations's oldest continuously performing arts organization, gives first concert.

1822 Boston is incorporated as a city.

1831 William Lloyd Garrison publishes an abolitionist journal, *The Liberator.*

1845 The writer Henry David Thoreau begins living at Walden Pond.

1846 General anesthesia first used at Massachusetts General Hospital.

1852 Boston Public Library, the first free city library, opens.

1857 Filling of Back Bay begins, cleaning up a 580-acre (235-hectare) dump.

1861 Massachusetts Institute of Technology is granted charter.

1863 54th Massachusetts Voluntary Infantry, the first African-American regiment, is formed. First American-style football played on Boston Common.

1868 Louisa May Alcott of Concord publishes *Little Women*.

1872 Great Fire of Boston kills 33 and destroys 776 buildings.

1876 First words are spoken over telephone by Alexander Graham Bell.

1879 Radcliffe College founded for women.

1881 Boston Symphony Orchestra founded. Frederick Law Olmsted begins work on Emerald Necklace park system.

1886 Henry James's *The Bostonians* published.

1897 Boston Marathon starts. First subway in America opens at Park Street.

1903 Boston Pilgrims defeat Pittsburgh Pirates in first baseball World Series.

1909 Filene's Automatic Bargain Basement opens in Washington Street.

1919 Strike of 1,300 Boston police. Breaking it brings Massachusetts Governor Calvin Coolidge to prominence.

1920 Red Sox sell Babe Ruth to New York Yankees for $125,000.

1927 Italian immigrants Nicola Sacco and Bartolomeo Vanzetti are executed in a Charlestown prison for alleged killings, a model case for social injustice.

1944 The computer age dawns in Cambridge laboratories as a 50-ft-long calculating machine gets its sums right.

1945 James Michael Curley wins fourth term as mayor.

1946 John Fitzgerald Kennedy, 29, elected to Congress.

1947 Edwin Land demonstrates first Polaroid camera in Cambridge.

1953 The world's first kidney transplant is performed at Brigham Hospital.

1955 Martin Luther King is awarded a PhD from Boston University.

1959 The Boston Redevelopment Authority begins razing the old West End and starts building Government Center and luxury apartments.

1962 The 'Boston Strangler' begins a 21-month rape and murder spree, killing 13 women.

1973 Robert Parker publishes *The Godwulf Manuscript*, the first 'Spenser' detective novel.

1978 A blizzard dumps 27.1 inches (69 cm) of snow on Boston, with drifts up to 15 ft (4.5 meters).

1985 Court mandated cleanup of Boston Harbor begins.

1990 In the largest art heist in history, thieves remove $200 million in paintings from Isabella Stewart Gardner Museum.

1991 The mammoth Third Harbor Tunnel/Central Artery Project begins.

2001 Two passenger airliners are hijacked from Logan Airport by terrorists and crashed into New York City's World Trade Center, killing 3,000.

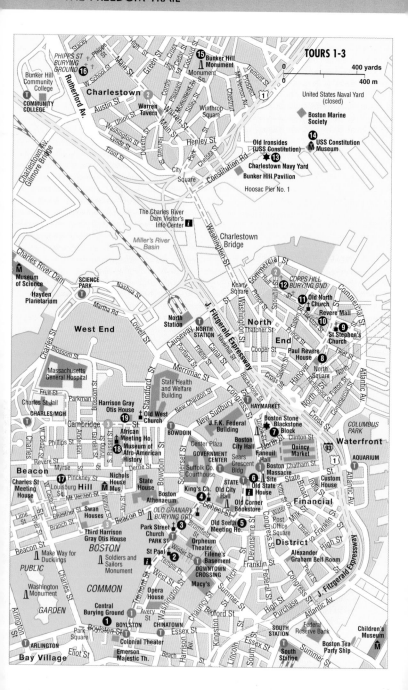

1: The Freedom Trail: Downtown Boston

The city's trademark attraction, the **Freedom Trail** is a 3-mile journey through the heart of Boston marked by a red line (sometimes painted, sometimes made of brick) that takes in 16 historic sites from **Boston Common** to the **Bunker Hill Monument** in Charlestown. The official starting point is a **Visitor Information Center** on the Tremont Street side of Boston Common, about 150 yards from the Park Street MBTA subway station. It has free maps and tour information. Located directly opposite the **Old State House**, the **Boston National Historical Park Visitor Center**, 15 State Street (tel: 242-5642) also has free maps and information as well as public restrooms.

> **The Freedom Trail**
> The 3-mile (5-km) Freedom Trail is a walking tour marked with a clear red line, which covers 16 historic buildings, sites and monuments that outline Boston's contribution to American history. Maps and brochures are available at the Boston Common Visitor Kiosk (tel: 536-5100) at 147 Tremont Street.

WALKING THROUGH HISTORY

Free guided walking tours by Park Service Rangers are offered in spring, summer and fall. Eight of the Freedom Trail sites – Bunker Hill Monument, Charlestown Navy Yard, Paul Revere House, Old North Church, Faneuil Hall, Old State House, and Old South Meeting House – lie within the Boston National Historical Park.

In 1951, Boston newspaper reporter William Greenough Schofield conceived the idea of a 'Freedom Trail', in order to rescue tourists who otherwise became lost in the city's notoriously disorderly colonial-era streetscape. Contrary to legend, those meandering thoroughfares were not originally cow paths – though, at one time, Boston Common was the city's common pasture. The original nexus of Boston in the 17th century was an open-air market at what is now the Old State House, then a short walk from the town dock (various landfill projects have progressively extended the distance to the waterfront). As the Puritan settlement grew, cobblestone paths radiated haphazardly from Great Street (now State Street).

Modern urban planning was then unknown, of course; instead, this 'city in a wilderness' grew organically, like a tree pushing out new branches.

Previous pages: the skyline across Charles River
Below: the State House

Map on page 18

If the early Bostonians gave any serious thought at all to how their new home should appear, they modeled it on the medieval English towns they had left behind.

BOSTON COMMON

A complete tour of the Freedom Trail may run anywhere from a one-hour express walk to a lingering one-day promenade, depending on one's energy and interests. By no means, however, does the Freedom Trail include every site worth visiting in the Cradle of Liberty. In fact, because it focuses almost exclusively on the Colonial and Revolutionary War periods, the Freedom Trail sometimes passes without a glance points of interest from relatively more recent times.

Below: Boston Common
Bottom: Park Street subway

In this book, two walking routes cover those sites as well as the stops on the Freedom Trail. The first route is confined to the central area of downtown Boston; the second takes in the North End and Charlestown.

★ ★ ★ **Boston Common**, where the Freedom Trail originates, is America's oldest public park; it covers some 48 acres (19 hectares) bounded by Park, Tremont, Boylston and Beacon streets. In 1630, the Common was created as a militia training grounds and 'for the feeding of Cattel' when the Puritans moved to Shawmut Peninsula from their original settlement at Charlestown. Troubled by a brackish water supply, they accepted the generous invitation of William Blackstone, then Shawmut's solitary settler, to share his 'excellent spring.' Blackstone lived here in a log cabin where he read his books and tended a vegetable garden and apple orchard. But, just as he had grown weary of 'the Lord Bishops' in England, so Blackstone soon grew tired of 'the Lord Brethren' in Boston. Preferring his own company, he left in 1635 and made a new settlement.

He would likely have been appalled to learn that the Puritans later installed on his former homestead their gallows, stocks and pillory where criminals, Quakers and witches were punished and executed.

PARK AND TREMONT STREETS

At the corner of Park and Tremont streets, the **Park Street subway** station was opened in 1897. Boston's underground trolleys were the first in the US and were intended to clear a constant log-jam of pedestrians and streetcars along Tremont Street. Originally, the subway ran just one stop to Boylston Station. The MBTA (Massachusetts Bay Transportation Authority, known as the 'T' for short) was set up in the 1960s to coordinate Boston's growing transportation network.

Central Burying Ground ❶ at the Boylston Street edge of the Common is the final resting place of many Revolutionary Patriots and British soldiers who perished at Bunker Hill; they lie here side by side in unmarked graves. Gilbert Stuart, the portrait painter whose depiction of George Washington is one of the most famous images in American art, died penniless and was also buried here in an unmarked vault.

Of the Common's various monuments, the most attractive – and the most significant – is the ★ ★ ★ **Robert Gould Shaw Memorial** (on the corner of Park and Beacon streets), which commemorates the bravery of the African-American soldiers of the 54th Massachusetts Regiment. Named for the 26-year-old white abolitionist who died in the mud with half his men in an 1863 attack on Fort Wagner, South Carolina, the

Star Attractions
● **Boston Common**
● **Robert Gould Shaw Memorial**

Hungry years
Located on the corner of Washington and School streets, the Boston Irish Famine Memorial remembers a famine that took the lives of more than a million people between 1845 and 1849. The memorial juxtaposes twin sculptures by artist Robert Shure; the first depicts an Irish family in the depths of despair during the famine, and the other illustrates their joyful new life in Boston.

The view from Boston Common

Map on page 18

bas-relief by Augustus Saint-Gaudens depicts Shaw on horseback surrounded by his troops. Though the memorial was commissioned in 1883 and dedicated in 1897, the names of the black soldiers who perished were not added until 1982.

THE STATE HOUSE

On July 4, 1795, Massachusetts Governor Samuel Adams and fellow patriot Paul Revere laid the cornerstone for the 'new' ★★★ **State House** (open Mon–Fri 10am–3.30pm; tel: 727-3676 for information about free guided tours given daily). The site, on Beacon Street overlooking Boston Common, was purchased from John Hancock whose mansion, since destroyed, stood nearby.

Below and bottom: views of the State House

The State House's principal entrance lies at the top of a flight of stairs, but there is also a public entrance at the Park Street side, near the **statue of General Joseph Hooker**, a Civil War commander. Beside him is the **statue of Mary Dyer**, who was hanged on Boston Common in 1660 for her Quaker beliefs. On the opposite lawn, the **statue of John Fitzgerald Kennedy** calls up the gallant side of America's youngest president.

Situated at 10½ Beacon Street is the **Boston Athenaeum** (tel: 227-0270), one of the nation's oldest private libraries, whose holdings encompass most of George Washington's own library.

Incorporated in 1807 and modeled after Palladio's Palazzo da Porta Festa in Vincenza, Italy, the library's holdings include books from the collection of Henry Knox, a bookseller who gained notoriety in the Revolutionary War by transporting cannons across Massachusetts.

Star Attraction
● State House

BULFINCH'S LEGACY

America's first professional architect, Charles Bulfinch, designed the red-brick and gold-domed State House when he was 24 years old. It is thought that his inspiration was Somerset House in London. For the construction, the state legislature appropriated £8,000, but the final bill came to more than four times the original estimate. In return for their money, Massachusetts' citizens received a magnificent work of architecture. A late 19th-century amendment of yellow-bricked wings to either side of the Bulfinch structure prompted one critic to liken the State House to a ham sandwich; but, despite this and other alterations, it remains one of the country's finest public buildings.

Doric Hall, the main room on the ground floor, has a portrait by Copley of General Thomas Gage, commander of British forces during the siege of Boston. The **Hall of Flags** displays the standards of state regiments from various wars. In the House of Representatives hangs the '**sacred codfish**,' a reminder of the importance Cape Cod fishery played in the early history of Massachusetts.

THE CATHEDRAL

Return to Boston Common at Park Street Station and cross Tremont Street to **St Paul's Cathedral-Episcopal ❷**, 138 Tremont (tel: 482-5800). The Greek Revival structure, by Alexander Parris (who also designed Quincy Market), was built in 1819–20; funds ran out before work for an entablature on the pediment could begin. At the corner of Tremont and Park Street, the 1809 **Park Street Church**, One Park Street (services on Sun at 8.30am, 11.30am, 4.30pm and 7pm; tel: 523-3383), was the last major Georgian church built

> **Native converts**
> In 1646, the General Court of Massachusetts passed an Act for the Propagation of the Gospel among the region's Native Americans. On October 28, Reverend John Eliot preached his first sermon to Native Americans in their own language in the wigwam of Waban, who became the first convert of his tribe in Nonantum (near Newton, Massachusetts).

General Joseph Hooker

Map on page 18

in Boston. Its prominent steeple rises 217 ft (66 meters). *America*, a hymn to the nation's 'spacious skies and amber waves of grain,' was first sung here on July 4, 1831.

HISTORICAL LUMINARIES

Beside Park Street Church is the ★★★ **Old Granary Burying Ground ❸**, which takes its name from a public granary that stood here. Revolutionary War heroes John Hancock, Samuel Adams, Paul Revere, Robert Treat Paine and James Otis lie buried here, along with the parents of Benjamin Franklin (marked by an obelisk in the center of the graveyard) and the victims of the Boston Massacre.

Below: Park Street Church
Bottom: Old Granary Burying Ground

Continue along Tremont away from Boston Common. On the opposite side of the street across from the Parker House Hotel, at the corner of School Street, is ★★ **King's Chapel ❹**, 58 Tremont Street (tel: 523-1749). Built in 1754 of Quincy granite, King's Chapel holds the largest of Paul Revere's bells, cast at the Revere Foundry in 1816. (Though best known for his 'midnight ride', Paul Revere was also a successful metal worker – he set up an iron and brass foundry in 1787.) The bell is still rung by hand today for all church services and special occasions. The severe, block-like exterior of the chapel conceals a superb Georgian style nave.

Boston's oldest graveyard, **King's Chapel Burying Ground**, includes among its permanent residents John Winthrop, first governor of Massachusetts, as well as Rev. John Cotton, a prominent Puritan minister, and the architect Charles Bulfinch. A modern plaque marks the grave of Elizabeth Pain, who was imprisoned for adultery and may have been Nathaniel Hawthorne's inspiration for Hester Prynne in *The Scarlet Letter*.

OLD CITY HALL

School Street is so named because it was the site of the original Boston Latin School, the nation's oldest public school (the current school build-

ing is in the Fenway near Children's Hospital).
A sidewalk plaque commemorating the Latin
School's founding in 1635 is located directly in
front of **Old City Hall**, designed in the French
Second Empire style and completed in 1862.
When city government offices were transferred
to a 'new' City Hall in 1969, the building was
threatened with demolition but was eventually
rescued and restored with offices and a restaurant.

In front, a **statue of Benjamin Franklin** hon-
ors a Latin School graduate who left Boston for
Philadelphia in 1723.

HUB OF THE HUB

At the corner of School and Washington streets is
the well-preserved ★ **Boston Globe Store**, 3
School Street, dating from 1712. As the Old
Corner Bookstore, it once housed Ticknor and
Fields, the publishers of Hawthorne, Thoreau,
Longfellow and Harriet Beecher Stowe. Between
1845 and 1865, the building was a meeting
ground of literary giants and was lionized as 'the
hub of the Hub' (as well as local lights, foreign
guests included Dickens and Thackeray). After it
had served as a pizza parlor in the 1960s, the
building was restored by the Boston Globe company. Today, the store sells books on New England and travel books.

Star Attractions
● Old Granary
Burying Ground
● King's Chapel

Sacred land
To ensure the presence of
the Church of England in
America, King James II ordered an
Anglican parish to be built in Boston.
When the colonists refused to sell any
suitable land, the king ordered the
Governor to seize a corner of the
burying ground for the Church of England, and it is here that the King's
Chapel was built. The Burying Ground
is the final resting place for, among
others, Mary Chilton, the first woman
to step off the Mayflower.

Store with a story to tell

MILK AND WASHINGTON STREETS

Diagonally opposite the Globe Corner Bookstore is the ★★**Old South Meeting House** ❺, 310 Washington Street (open daily 10am–4pm; tel: 482-6439). The Boston Tea Party began here on the night of December 16, 1773, when Sam Adams gave a signal during a meeting of the Sons of Liberty. The crowd began to whoop and make other warlike cries, then poured out into the streets and headed for the city's wharves (*see page 9*). Old South, Boston's second oldest church, was built in 1729 by Congregationalists; during the siege of Boston it was occupied by British troops, who converted it into a riding school by ripping out the pews and covering the floor with sand. The Great Fire of 1872, which devoured a 65-acre (26-hectare) area from Washington Street to the waterfront, was stopped just outside its doors.

Below: Old South Meeting House
Bottom: Old State House

From the corner of Milk and Washington streets, walk two blocks north to State Street and arrive at the back of the recently restored ★★**Old State House** ❻, 206 Washington Street (open daily 9am–5pm; tel: 720-3290); here you will find permanent exhibits on the Revolutionary War period installed by the Bostonian Society, who lease the building from the city. Before entering, walk down State Street to the front end, facing Congress Street, in order to admire the figures of a lion and unicorn atop the gabled facade.

These symbols of British royalty, which were removed in a peak of patriotic frenzy in 1776 and later replaced, recall the days when the royal governors of Massachusetts presided here, beginning in 1713. The building later served as the first State House and as Boston City Hall from 1831 to 1840.

Visitors should note that the **US National Park Service Visitor Center**, located opposite the Old State House at 15 State Street, has public restrooms, which are rare along the Freedom Trail.

THE BOSTON MASSACRE

On a traffic island in front of the Old State House is a **memorial to the Boston Massacre,** at the site where an unruly mob confronted a band of trigger-happy redcoats on March 5, 1770 and five Bostonians fell dead. As they prepared to leave Boston for battle in the Civil War, the all-black 54th Regiment paused here to pay their respects to Crispus Attucks, an African-American who was among those killed in the massacre.

LIBERTY AND UNION

Follow Congress Street north one block. On the left-hand side is the back of the 'new' ★ **City Hall**, which was opened in 1969 following nearly a decade of controversial urban renewal that leveled Scollay Square, a famed vaudeville district, to make way for a **Government Center**, a complex of city, state and federal office buildings.

Architects are among the few to praise City Hall, a brick and concrete pile in the Brutalist style by Kallman, McKinnel & Knowles; Bostonians love to hate the building for its outlandish appearance (by local standards) and for its incomprehensible floor plans. An obscure plaque on City Hall Plaza notes that Alexander Graham Bell and Thomas Watson perfected the telephone in a building long since razed.

Much more to everyone's liking is ★ ★ **Faneuil Hall**, on Congress Street opposite. Behind a statue of Samuel Adams, with arms folded in determined opposition to British tyranny, stands the

> **Devastating disease**
> Between 1616 and 1617, a smallpox epidemic introduced by European traders wiped out nearly one-third of the New England coast's native Wampanoag tribe, and put the coastal tribes at the mercy of their inland enemies. So intense was the devastation at some Wampanoag villages that settlers found only bones scattered in the ground, because there was no one left to bury the dead.

Faneuil Hall

Map on page 18

familiar brick building with white cupola and grasshopper weather vane. Faneuil Hall was first built as a central market in 1742 with money donated by merchant Peter Faneuil (the French name recalls his Huguenot origins and may be pronounced either as Fan'l or Fan-u-el). Faneuil was described by John Hancock as 'the topmost merchant in all the town.'

Following a fire in 1761, it was rebuilt in the same design, then altered and enlarged by Charles Bulfinch in 1805. The years leading up to the Revolutionary War heard speeches given here by James Otis and Samuel Adams, among others, and in the years after independence, Faneuil Hall hosted gala balls honoring Washington and Lafayette. On the first floor are shops and a US post office. The **Assembly Room** is dominated by a painting, *Liberty and Union, Now and Forever*, that shows Daniel Webster forcefully declaiming in the US Senate; the hall is still used today for political debates and citizenship ceremonies for naturalized immigrants.

Below and bottom: fun, food and leisure at Faneuil Hall

QUINCY MARKET

By 1822, when Boston was incorporated as a city, Bostonians had outgrown the market facilities provided at Faneuil Hall. Mayor Josiah Quincy, known as 'the great Mayor,' sought and won approval for a new market; his fellow citizens eventually named the market after him. ★★★ **Quincy Market**, directly behind Faneuil Hall, consists of three long and slender buildings designed by Alexander Parris in 1824. The **Central Building**, made of granite with a central, copper-clad rotunda, is flanked by the brick warehouses of **North Market** and **South Market**. In the early 1970s, following a long period of decline, Faneuil Hall and Quincy Market were restored and revitalized as a so-called 'festival marketplace', bustling with shops, restaurants, comedy clubs and bars.

The great success of the project led to its imitation across the United States and around the world. Today, Faneuil Hall Marketplace, as it is known, is rivaled as a tourist attraction only by the likes of Disneyland, and is visited by an estimated 50,000 people daily.

Return to the aisle between Faneuil Hall and Quincy Market, a popular performance space for musicians, mimes and jugglers, and cross North Street to Union Street. On a long traffic island between Congress and Union streets are ★ **two statues** dedicated to James Michael Curley, who served four terms as Mayor of Boston, the first in 1914 and the last in 1945 (a race he won in a landslide while under federal indictment), as well as stints as Massachusetts Governor and US Congressman. The statues – one seated, the other standing – depict 'His Honor' in his dual role as man of the people and great orator.

HOLOCAUST MEMORIAL

Further down the island, set on a black granite path, is the line of 6 luminous towers that constitute the ★ ★ **New England Holocaust Memorial**, which commemorates the 6 million Jews who died in Nazi death camps. Erected in 1985 by sculptor Stanley Saitowitz, each of the 54-foot (16-meter) towers are lit internally to gleam at night, and bear the name of one of the six major death camps – Auschwitz-Birkenau, Chelmno, Sobibor, Treblinka, Majdanek and Belzec.

Star Attractions
● **Quincy Market**
● **New England Holocaust Memorial**

Boston memories
Amid the crowds of tourists, the Faneuil Hall Heritage Shop is relatively quiet – its basement location keeps the hordes away. But here, in Boston's oldest pewter store, you will find souvenirs with a difference. Selling pewter, scrimshaw, jewelry and hand-crafted artifacts, it's open Mon–Sat 11am–7pm, Sun 11am–5pm (tel: 723-1776).

Shopping at Quincy Market

BLACKSTONE BLOCK

Cross Union Street to **Ye Olde Union Oyster House** (open Sun–Thur 11am–9.30pm, Fri and Sat 11am–10pm; tel: 227-2750); this is Boston's oldest restaurant, dating from 1826, where you can still eat traditional New England dishes. Now turn right down Salt Lane into the **Blackstone Block ❼**. Named for Boston's first settler, this compact collection of brick buildings and narrow alleys is the city's oldest commercial block.

Street names such as Creek Square and Marsh Lane are a reminder that what is now dry land once lay on the water's edge. The brick building at 10 Marshall Street was constructed in 1760 by Thomas Hancock, John's uncle, and was later owned by John's brother, Ebenezer. Built in 1714, 41 Union Street is the oldest building. Its second story was home to the *Massachusetts Spy*, the newspaper of the Whig patriots from 1771 to 1775. Louis Philippe, who ruled France from 1830 to 1848, eked out a living teaching French in his second-floor bedroom. Ye Old Union Oyster House is in the same building.

Below and bottom: street scenes

STONE MARKER

On the opposite side, at the corner of Salt Lane, the ★ **Boston Stone** lies at street level in a building foundation. The stone was shipped here from England in 1700 for a paint mill and laid here in 1737 by a tavern owner. It was later used as the point from which all distances to Boston were measured on roadside mile markers.

On Fridays and Saturdays, the Blackstone Block buzzes with the activity of the **Haymarket**, when fishmongers, butchers and produce peddlers sell their goods and create a lively and colorful street theater.

At the intersection of Hanover and Blackstone Streets, bronze reliefs of newspapers, food and other market detritus are embedded into the street pavement. Called ★ **Asaraton**, from the ancient Greek for unswept floors, the sculpture is surely the city's oddest and most easily overlooked work of public art.

BOSTON & MAINE FISH COMPANY

THE LOBSTER BAR

2: The Freedom Trail: North End and Charlestown

This tour begins in the North End and concludes in Charlestown. Five Freedom Trail sites are located here, as well as other important points of interest. To reach the North End, cross under the elevated Fitzgerald Expressway (or 'Central Artery'), through a pedestrian tunnel from Blackstone Street in Haymarket *(see facing page)* to the intersection of Salem and Cross Streets.

Those who prefer not to walk may travel directly to the Charlestown Navy Yard and *USS Constitution* via the Route 93 MBTA bus from Haymarket station (one block from Blackstone Street at New Sudbury Street). In addition, a water shuttle operated by Boston Harbor Cruises (tel: 227-4320; $1 each way) leaves Long Wharf (between the Marriott Long Wharf Hotel and the New England Aquarium) for the Navy Yard every 30 minutes (15 minutes on weekday morning and evening rush hours).

> **The Big Dig**
> Visitors and Bostonians can look forward to the eventual removal of the unsightly Central Artery, which will be replaced by an underground highway as part of the major construction works going on here (called the Big Dig). In the meantime, expect disruption on a large scale. More details: page 49.

NORTH END

Associated today with Italian cafés and restaurants, the North End's unique character and geographic isolation make the area seem like an urban island. The **Central Artery**, constructed in the

Paul Revere's Mall

Map
on page
18

Little Italy tours
Michel Topor, an authority on Italian food, wine and culture, leads walking tours through Little Italy on Wednesdays and Saturdays at 10am and 2pm, and on Fridays at 3pm. Reservations are required; tel: 523-6032.

Below: Italian Quarter
Bottom: Paul Revere statue

1950s, has much to do with this, of course. The elevated roadway presents pedestrians with a wall of girders, concrete and pavement that can be crossed in a limited number of places. Nevertheless, the district's isolation is historic. In the 17th century, the North End was linked to Shawmut Peninsula by a narrow neck (the present Blackstone Street) and was even known as the 'island of North Boston.'

GOOD EATING

From the 1820s, the North End has been a stronghold for waves of immigrant populations. First the Irish, then Eastern European Jews, and now Italians have found the North End an ideal setting to establish a distinctive American community with strong ties to the old country.

Exit the pedestrian walkway from Haymarket *(see above)*, turn right on Cross Street, left on Hanover Street, right on Prince Street to North Square; this short walk passes numerous restaurants, cafés and Italian food shops. A trip to the North End isn't complete without stopping for an espresso in a café, a slice of pizza at Pizzeria Regina *(see page 103)*, or a meal at any one of two dozen restaurants in the area. On summer weekends, the North End's narrows streets are crowded for the sort of colorful festivals and religious processions usually seen only on Italian soil.

HISTORIC HOMES

A sightseeing tour through the North End traditionally begins at the ★ ★ **Paul Revere House 8**, 19 North Square (open Tues–Sun 9.30am–4.15pm; admission fee; tel: 523-1676), which the famous patriot owned from 1770 to 1800 *(see also page 74)*. Built in 1680, the clapboard house with diamond-shaped casement windows is the oldest in Boston and lies behind a high wooden fence. A half-ton **bronze bell** – one of 200 bells made at Paul Revere's foundry – stands in the front courtyard. In addition to his well-known equestrian duties on April 18, 1775, Revere was a master silversmith, metallurgist and engraver of Huguenot descent (his father, Apollos de Rivoire, fled to Boston from France in 1715 and anglicized his name to Paul Revere).

Exhibits inside the Revere House, which became a museum in 1907, include the **saddle bags** Revere used on his midnight ride plus a variety of 17th- and 18th-century furnishings.

Beside the Paul Revere House on the same grounds is the Georgian-style **Pierce-Hichborn House** (tel: 523-1676 for guided tour information), built in 1711 by glazier Moses Pierce, and now the oldest brick building in Boston. Nathaniel Hichborn, Paul Revere's cousin, bought the home in 1781 and it remained in the family until 1864.

St Stephen's

Backtrack to Hanover Street and then turn right. ★ ★ **St Stephen's Church** , 24 Clark Street (tel: 523-1230), is at the corner of Hanover and Clark streets. Now a Roman Catholic church, St Stephen's was designed by the ubiquitous Charles Bulfinch and built in 1804 of red brick with a prominent white tower. This is his only surviving church in Boston, and was by turns a Congregational meeting house and the Second Unitarian Church of Boston until the Catholic Diocese purchased it in 1862. Directly opposite St Stephen's

Star Attractions
- **Paul Revere House**
- **St Stephen's Church**

Below: St Stephen's Church
Bottom: Paul Revere House

is ★★★**Paul Revere Mall ❿**, also known as the **Prado**. Beneath an **equestrian statue** of Revere by Cyrus Dallin, local residents gather to relax and share gossip (in English and Italian). Continue to the far end of the mall and across Unity Street.

OLD NORTH CHURCH

*Below and bottom:
Old North Church*

Built in 1723, **Old North Church ⓫** (formally Christ Church), 193 Salem Street (open daily 9am–5pm; tel: 523-4848 or 800-981-4776) is Boston's oldest and most famous church. The steeple is the most recent in a series of replacements due to hurricanes and fires.

The bells were cast in Gloucester, England, and hung in 1745; as a young boy, Paul Revere was a member of a guild that rang the bells. On April 18, 1775, as British troops began crossing the Charles to Cambridge, the church sexton, Robert Newman, followed Paul Revere's orders and climbed the tower to hang two lanterns that could be seen in Charlestown as an alarm signal.

An active Episcopal Church today, every Sunday the oldest maiden peal of bells in North America are rung. The organ case is a descendant of the first organ built in the colonies, and can be heard weekly at the 11am Sunday service and often at the 5pm Second Sunday concert. Inside the church, where Revere's descendants still main-

tain a family pew, is a **bust of George Washington** at the rear of the apse. On a visit in 1824, French General Lafayette, who served as the Virginian's aide-de-camp, admired the bust as 'more like him than any other portrait.' Behind the church's Clough House is a meticulously maintained garden, with exotic flowers dating back to the colonial era. Fifty-minute guided tours of the Old North Campus are offered hourly from June to October, and begin at the Clough House.

SECOND CEMETERY

At the entrance of Old North Church, facing Hull Street, walk straight to **Copp's Hill Burying Ground** ⑫ (1659), Boston's second oldest cemetery and named for William Copp, who farmed on the hill in the 1640s. Look for the impressions of musket balls on many of the tombstones, left when British troops practiced their marksmanship here in the Revolutionary War period.

Near the gate at the Charter Street edge of the cemetery is the **Mather Tomb**, last resting place of Increase and Cotton Mather, father and son, as well as numerous others in the famous family of Puritan ministers. Cotton Mather is remembered for helping incite the Salem 'Witch Trials' in 1692 – he wrote *The Wonders of the Invisible World*, a catalog of witchcraft and demonry – but Mather also helped urge a great advance in science when he convinced Boston physician Zabdiel Boylston to use inoculation as a way of protecting citizens during a 1721 smallpox epidemic (the minister had read about inoculation theory in English scientific journals). The corner of the graveyard at Snowhill Street was the **precinct for deceased blacks**, including Prince Hall, first grand master of the African Grand Lodge of Masons in Massachusetts.

CHARLESTOWN

From Copp's Hill Burying Ground, follow Charter Street to Commercial Street and cross to the water's edge. Turn left and continue several

Star Attraction
● Paul Revere Mall

Language tours
Don Quijote Tours conduct daily Spanish-speaking tours of Boston or outlying areas. Tours are also available in French, Portuguese and Italian. Telephone 328-1333 for more information.

Copp's Hill Burying Ground

Map on page 18

Free tours
Boston's Parks and Recreation Department Park Rangers (1010 Massachusetts Avenue) offer a number of free tours and programs. Telephone 635-7383 for information, schedules and meeting locations.

blocks to Endicott Street and the Boston side of the Charlestown bridge. Turn right and cross the bridge, which lies over the terminus of a series of locks linking the Charles River with Boston Harbor. The red line of the Freedom Trail as well as a series of signs will direct you along Constitution Road to the *USS Constitution* and the Charlestown Navy Yard, through an otherwise uninteresting (to a degree even unappealing) district of warehouses and highway exit ramps.

As previously mentioned, a water shuttle operated by Boston Harbor Cruises (tel: 227-4320; $1 each way) leaves Long Wharf (between the Marriott Long Wharf Hotel and the New England Aquarium) for the Navy Yard every 30 minutes (every 15 minutes at weekday morning and evening rush hours). The short harbor trip represents an attractive alternative to walking.

THE NAVY YARD

The ★ ★ ★ **Charlestown Navy Yard** ⑬ (tel: 242-5601) was for over 160 years one of the country's most important naval centers, from its opening during the War of 1812 to its closing in 1974 as the Vietnam War drew to an end. Perhaps the most unusual structure on the 30-acre (12-hectare) site is the quarter-mile **rope-walk**, where ships'

USS Constitution

cordage was produced; it was designed by Alexander Parris, architect of Quincy Market, and completed in 1837. The Charlestown Navy Yard's prime attraction is the ★ ★ ★ *USS Constitution* (open Thur–Sun noon–4pm; free admission; tel: 242-5670), the oldest commissioned ship in the US Navy. The vessel has been completely refurbished. Navy seamen dressed in uniforms from the War of 1812 lead guided tours of the cramped living quarters below deck. Launched in 1797 from Edmund Hartt's North End shipyard, at 204 ft (62 meters) long, with a displacement of 2,200 tons, she was the largest frigate of her kind. Paul Revere cast the bolts fastening its timbers as well as the copper sheathing for the ship's bottom.

When Congress declared war on the Barbary States of North Africa in 1802, the Constitution played a leading role in the blockade and bombardment of Tripoli. When Congress again declared war in 1812, this time against the British, the ship gained immortal fame while under the leadership of Captain Isaac Hull in a contest with the Royal Navy frigate, *Guerriere*. During a fierce skirmish that saw the two ships approach within pistol firing range, a British cannonball appeared to bounce off the oak hull of the *Constitution*. 'Good God,' an American sailor exclaimed, 'her sides are made of iron!' An hour later, the *Guerriere* surrendered and the *Constitution* became known as Old Ironsides. In over 84 years of active service, the floating fortress won 42 battles, lost none, and captured 20 vessels.

OLD IRONSIDES

The *Constitution* fought her last fight in 1815, and in 1830 the navy made plans to scrap the ship. Oliver Wendell Holmes (then a Harvard law student) penned his poem 'Old Ironsides', which was published in newspapers across the nation. The resulting public outcry saved the ship. In 1897, Congressman John 'Honey Fitz' Fitzgerald again prevailed upon Congress to cough up money for much needed repairs. The ship was rescued once more in the late 1920s by a children's campaign

Star Attractions
- Charlestown Navy Yard
- USS Constitution

Below and bottom: on board the USS Constitution

Map on page 18

Below: Old Ironsides
Bottom: Bunker Hill Monument

of pennies and nickels, and has been berthed at the Charlestown Navy Yard ever since. Every July 4, the ship takes a majestic turn in Boston Harbor so that its hardy hull will weather evenly.

The floating companion of Old Ironsides is the *USS Cassin Young*, a decommissioned World War II destroyer. The ★★ **USS Constitution Museum** ⑭ (open daily 10am–5pm; free admission; tel: 426-1812) details the ship's history and the lives of its sailors, and features a theater, interactive exhibits, historical artifacts, gallery tours, and a gift shop. A variety of ship's models and paintings of clipper ships are displayed at the nearby **Boston Marine Society** (tel: 242-0522).

BUNKER HILL MONUMENT

Pick up the red line of the Freedom Trail outside the Navy Yard and follow it up Monument Avenue to the 221-ft (67-meter) high ★★★ **Bunker Hill Monument** ⑮ (open daily 9am–4.30pm; free admission; tel: 242-5641), dedicated on July 17, 1843 by President John Tyler. Daniel Webster, Tyler's Secretary of State, delivered a thundering oration to a crowd of 100,000.

Energetic visitors can ascend the 294 steps for a view of Charlestown and Boston harbor (there is no elevator). A museum at the base of the monument includes dioramas of one of the first major

battles in the Revolutionary War. The Battle of Bunker Hill, as it is known, in fact took place on Breed's Hill, which is also the location of the Bunker Hill Monument.

The fault, if that's the word, lies with Colonel William Prescott and his men, who were ordered on June 16, 1775 by General Artemus Ward of the Continental Army to fortify Bunker Hill, but chose instead to dig in at Breed's. This was probably not accidental, for Breed's Hill was lower and lay closer to Boston than Bunker Hill. What the Yankees sought was a commanding position overlooking Boston harbor; for their pains, they attracted punishing shelling by the British fleet on the morning of June 17. Later, a force of 1,500 Redcoats landed at Charlestown and set fire to the nearly deserted district.

FALLEN HEROES

When the British began a charge up Breed's Hill that afternoon, the Yankees held their fire until the enemy came within 50 feet (15 meters). The delaying tactic was prompted by a need to conserve ammunition, but it has given rise to the legend that Colonel Prescott ordered his men, 'Don't fire till you see the whites of their eyes!' In fact, the remark was already something of a military cliché. The Battle of Bunker Hill took a bloody toll on both sides. Among the 140 Americans who died was Dr Joseph Warren, recently commissioned a major-general; Major John Pitcairn fell along with 225 other Redcoats. Wounded were 271 Americans and 828 British.

THE MONUMENT'S ORIGINS

Designed by Simon Willard and built of Quincy granite, the Bunker Hill Monument's cornerstone was laid on June 17, 1825 (the 50th anniversary of the battle) by General Lafayette. Funding and engineering problems caused interminable construction delays over the next 13 years, and a private railway for horse-drawn carts – America's first commercial railway – hauled from Quincy

Star Attraction
● Bunker Hill Monument

JFK Crossing
Near President John F. Kennedy's birthplace, now called JFK Crossing, an ethnic community thrives with its own unique identity. A flourishing Jewish community has long been a force here, with numerous kosher restaurants, bagel shops and specialty food stores. Bookstores and art galleries also abound in the area.

Bunker Hill Monumnent

Map on page 18

Below and bottom: Warren Tavern

to Boston the extraordinarily heavy blocks called for in Willard's design. Descend Monument Avenue to Warren Street, turn right and take the next left onto Pleasant Street. The three-story **Warren Tavern**, 2 Pleasant Street (tel: 241-8142) is the oldest tavern in Boston (built in 1780 after the Charlestown fire) and was named for the fallen hero of the Battle of Bunker Hill. Among the patriots who once stopped here were Paul Revere and General George Washington.

FIRST SETTLERS' GRAVES

Where Warren Street meets Main Street at Thompson Square, continue to Phipps Street on the left and turn into the ★ **Phipps Street Burying Ground** ⓰, which provides the best historical record of pre-revolutionary Charlestown: families were buried in rectangular plots corresponding to the locations of their homes. Although John Harvard is not actually buried here, an obelisk commemorating the preacher was erected in 1828 by Harvard alumni. When he died in 1638, he left his books and half his estate to a new college established by the Puritans which was later named in his honor. Many of Boston's first generation of settlers are also buried in the cemetery; at least 100 graves date from before 1700.

You can now return to the center of Boston via

3: Beacon Hill

In 1630, the most prominent feature of Shaw-mut Peninsula was Trimountaine, so named for its three peaks: Pemberton, Beacon and Mount Vernon (looking from east to west). Today, only a truncated Beacon Hill survives, with the others leveled for various landfill projects that accommodated Boston's swelling population in the 18th and 19th centuries.

MAPPING THE FUTURE

As early as 1634, an act of legislation designated Beacon Hill as a sentry spot, and a torch was left blazing there to guide ships safely into Boston Harbor. Beacon Hill began to acquire its current appearance in 1795, when Samuel Adams, then Massachusetts governor, and Paul Revere laid the cornerstone for a new State House designed by Charles Bulfinch. Shortly afterward, Harrison Gray Otis and other prominent local merchants formed the Mount Vernon Proprietors to buy and develop land in the surrounding area. They began with a vast parcel owned by artist John Single-ton Copley, making for the largest land transaction in Boston up to that time, covering an area enclosed by Beacon Street, Walnut Street, Mount Vernon Street to Louisbourg Square, down Pinckney to what was then the Charles River and along its bank to Beacon Street. The Proprietors immediately began to lay out streets and construct a series of mansions and townhouses which form an architectural legacy equaled in Boston only by the later development of Back Bay.

PRIME REAL ESTATE

Beacon Hill is noteworthy not only for its buildings, however, but also for its inhabitants. If Boston was indeed the Athens of America in the 19th century, then 'the hill' was its Mount Olympus, home to such towering figures as Henry Adams, Louisa May Alcott, William Dean Howells, and Francis Parkman. The American

Below and bottom: residential preoccupations on the Hill

Map on page 18

Unitarian Association was formed here in 1825, and Unitarians on Beacon Hill and elsewhere played a large role in shaping the moral character of Bostonians. The Brahmins, as they became known, were serious, prosperous, and thoroughly patrician, yet among them were abolitionists, philosophers, and numerous men and women of *belles lettres*.

BEACON STREET

From the State House, Beacon Street slopes to the west along the edge of Boston Common. The **Unitarian Universalist Association**, a successor to the American Unitarian Association, has its offices at 25 Beacon Street (tel: 742-2100); its bookstore sells a full line of volumes from the UUA-owned Beacon Press. Joy Street, at the first crosswalk, dates from 1661 and is one of Boston's oldest streets. At 5 Joy Street are the headquarters of the **Appalachian Mountain Club** (tel: 523-0636), which maintains trails and shelters for hikers and mountaineers on the Appalachian Trail through the White Mountains of New Hampshire and elsewhere in New England.

Designed by Alexander Parris, architect of Quincy Market, the twin structures at 39 and 40 Beacon Street were built in 1819 for, respectively, Nathan Appleton, a merchant, and Daniel

Below and bottom: Charles Street antique stores

Pinckney Parker, who owned stock in the Lowell mill concerns. Parris also designed the adjacent Sears Mansion, 42 Beacon Street, which is now the library and rooms of the exclusive **Somerset Club** (not open to the public). Here, original window panes are tinted purple from impurities in the glass that were sensitive to sunlight. Purple glass can also be seen at King's Chapel House, located at 64 Beacon Street.

In 1806, Harrison Gray Otis – whose long career of public service included terms as US Senator and Mayor of Boston – moved into ★ ★ **45 Beacon Street**, another fine building designed by Charles Bulfinch. The current occupants, the American Meteorological Society (tel: 227-2425), are required under the terms of their lease to show the mansion, where Otis entertained President James Monroe and many others, to anyone who so inquires.

REVEREND WILLIAM BLAXTON

Before turning up Spruce Street, take note of a plaque at 50 Beacon Street that recalls the memory of the 'Rev. William Blaxton,' who is credited as 'first settler of Shawmut 1625. Near here stood his dwelling… The Place of his Seclusion became a Great City.' Blackstone, as his name is usually written, was a graduate of Emanuel College, Cambridge, England and a member of a failed colony near what is now Weymouth.

In 1625, he agreed with the local inhabitants to take possession of the Shawmut peninsula, where he lived alone with his books and a vegetable garden until the arrival of the Puritans.

CHESTNUT STREET

Turn right on Spruce Street, then left on Chestnut Street, which along with Mt Vernon Street are the architectural jewels of Beacon Hill. During the Civil War, Dr Samuel Gridley Howe, founder of the Perkins Institute for the Blind, and his wife, author Julia Ward Howe, lived at ★ ★ **13 Chestnut Street**. In addition to their formidable

Star Attractions
- **45 Beacon Street**
- **13 Chestnut Street**

Shaping the city
When the Puritans arrived in Boston in the 17th century, grand hills dominated the landscape and uninhabitable wetlands limited development and commerce. Landfill projects were undertaken to reshape the city, the largest task being the filling in of Back Bay *(see page 54)*. Now one of Boston's only remaining hills, Beacon Hill's charms include cobblestone streets, gas lamps, fine19th-century townhouses and famous landmarks.

Chestnut Street windowbox

Map on page 18

professional careers, the couple were ardent abolitionists; Mrs Howe wrote the words to *The Battle Hymn of the Republic*, the rousing Union marching song. This house and numbers 15 and 17 were designed and built by Charles Bulfinch between 1816 and 1818. The brick facade, black shutters, and white columns at the entrances are quintessential Beacon Hill features.

The oldest home (1799) on the south slope of Beacon Hill is ★ **29A Chestnut Street**, also by Bulfinch; the curved frontage was added around 1820, and contains several panes of purple glass. As with the windows of the Somerset Club, this was caused by defective glass which coloured when exposed to sunlight. The actor Edwin Booth, brother of Lincoln's assassin John Wilkes Booth, lived here in the 1880s. The historian Francis Parkman lived at **50 Chestnut Street** from 1865 until 1893.

CHARLES STREET

At the bottom of Chestnut Street is **Charles Street**, the commercial center of Beacon Hill. The street is lined with boutiques and eclectic antique shops, and there are several good restaurants and cafés where one can buy Italian pastries, *gelato* and a stiff cup of espresso. At the corner of Charles and Mt Vernon streets, the **Charles Street**

Below: Chestnut Street brass
Bottom: Louisburg Square

Meeting House was built from a design by Asher Benjamin as the Third Baptist Church.

In 1807, the Charles River came near the church doorstep and baptisms were performed in its waters. Today, the church building is used for stores and offices.

LOUISBURG SQUARE

For many visitors today, ★★★**Louisburg Square** ⑰ (pronounced *Lew-is-burg*) is the high point of a Beacon Hill tour. The square's centerpiece is a private park enclosed by a wrought-iron fence. The park is maintained by the owners of the surrounding townhouses, who comprised the first home association in the United States. Statues of Columbus and Aristides the Just were donated in 1850 by Joseph Iasigi, a Greek merchant. Louisburg Square and its cobblestone streets have welcomed numerous famous residents in over a century and a half.

The area was named for the Siege of Louisburg, a Nova Scotia fortress captured by Massachusetts militiamen in 1754. William Dean Howells, novelist and editor of the *Atlantic Monthly*, once lived at No. 4; the writer Louisa May Alcott moved her parents and sisters to No. 10 after her success with *Little Women*; in 1852, Jenny Lind, the 'Swedish Nightingale,' married her accompanist at No. 20.

> **Gentrification**
> Visitors to Beacon Hill will notice that north of Pinckney Street, the houses are less grand. These buildings were once home to servants, sailors and former slaves; they later attracted artists and immigrants. Today, this area has been largely gentrified, and many former rooming houses have been converted into family homes.

Louisburg Square

MT VERNON STREET

Beacon Hill's finest homes line ★★**Mt Vernon Street**, which Henry James satirically tagged as 'the only respectable street in America.' The ★★**Second Harrison Gray Otis House** at 85 Mt Vernon Street, a three-story mansion with cobblestone drive, was built by Bulfinch in 1800–2. His dream of a group of free-standing homes never materialized, however. Henry Adams, author and historian, grew up at **57 Mt Vernon Street**, another of Bulfinch's distinguished contributions to this district.

At the top of the hill, the ★**Nichols House Museum**, 55 Mt Vernon Street (open May–Oct:

Tue–Sat 12–4pm; Nov–April: Thur, Fri, Sat 12–4pm; tel: 227-6993), is the only private house open as a museum to be found on Beacon Hill; Rose Nichols, the niece of Augustus Saint-Gaudens and a writer and landscape architect who died in 1960, was its last resident. The facade has not been altered since it was constructed by Charles Bulfinch in 1804.

UNDERGROUND RAILWAY

At the crest of Mt Vernon Street, turn left on Joy Street toward the **North Slope** of Beacon Hill, which was a predominantly African-American area in the 18th and 19th centuries. Many of the homes here are listed on Boston's **Black Heritage Trail**. On Pinckney Street, No. 62 was a stop on the '**Underground Railway**,' a chain of safe houses for slaves fleeing the South to freedom in Canada before the Civil War (even though Massachusetts and other Northern states had abolished slavery, the Fugitive Slave Act permitted the arrest and return of escaped blacks). In 1920, workers uncovered a secret attic chamber here, as well as a tin plate and two iron spoons.

Below: bikers on Joy Street
Bottom: 62 Pinckney Street

ABOLITIONISTS' BARBERS

The **John J. Smith House**, 86 Pinckney Street, is named for a free black from Virginia whose

barbershop at the site was a popular meeting place for African-American abolitionists. In 1878, Smith became the first African-American appointed to the Boston Common Council.

Backtrack to Joy Street, but pause at 24 Pinckney Street to see why it is known as the '**House of Odd Windows**' (each one is different, from a roof-top 'eyelid' window to a small square window beside the front door). Turn left on Joy Street and descend to **Smith Court**. The **Abiel Smith School**, 46 Joy Street, was dedicated in 1834 for the education of African-Americans, but was closed 10 years later when Boston's public schools became racially integrated.

Today, the school contains the offices of the ★★★**Museum of Afro-American History** ⑱ (open Mon–Sat 10am–4pm; tel: 739-1200), which maintains its exhibits at the neighboring **African Meeting House**, 8 Smith Court (tel: 742-5415). Dedicated in 1806, the African Meeting House is the oldest African-American church still standing. It was known as the 'haven from the loft' because black worshippers at Old North Church were confined to the loft. In 1832, William Lloyd Garrison, publisher of *The Liberator*, founded the New England Anti-Slavery Society here.

PRESERVATION SOCIETY

At the bottom of Joy Street, cross Cambridge Street and turn right to the headquarters of the Society for the Preservation of New England Antiquities (SPNEA), located in the distinguished ★★**First Harrison Gray Otis House** ⑲, 141 Cambridge Street (open Wed–Sun 11am–5pm; admission fee; tel: 227-3956).

Designed by Charles Bulfinch in 1796, this symmetrical three-storey red-brick structure is the most distinguished mansion still standing in Boston, and epitomizes the wealth of Boston's governing class after the Revolution. The interior has been refurbished with furniture and portraits from Federal times, with canary-yellow wallpaper and mirror-panneled doors. The basement contains an architectural museum.

Star Attractions
- Museum of Afro-American History
- First Harrison Gray Otis House

Black Heritage Trail
Free tours of the Black Heritage Trail are offered on weekdays at 10am, noon, and 2pm by reservation only. Tours begin at the Shaw Memorial and feature the African Meeting House, Abiel Smith School and George Middleton House. Call the Museum of Afro-American History (tel: 739-0022) or the Boston African-American National Historic Site (tel: 742-5415) to make reservations 24 hours in advance.

Acorn Street

Map on page 18

CAMBRIDGE STREET

Old West Church, 131 Cambridge Street (tel: 227-5088) was designed by Asher Benjamin in 1806 and is a Methodist church. A predecessor was destroyed in 1775 when the British thought the Americans were using its steeple to signal to their compatriots in Cambridge. Formerly known as the West End, the area behind and beside the church and Otis House was razed in the late 1950s for an urban renewal project that created the nearby Government Center and several high-rise apartment towers.

Backtrack along Cambridge Street toward the Charles River. Turn right on Grove Street, then left on to Fruit Street to the complex that constitutes Massachusetts General Hospital (known as MGH) and the grey-bricked **George R. White Memorial Building**, with its landmark bay window tower. In 1810, a committee led by Dr John Collins Warren raised more than $100,000 for construction of a public hospital; today, it is an internationally recognized medical institution.

Inside the hospital's main entrance, ask directions to the ★ **Bulfinch Pavilion and Ether Dome** (tel: 726-2000), an historic landmark twice over; firstly because it was Bulfinch's last Boston commission before he departed to become architect of the US Capitol, and secondly, because it was here ether was used for the first time (*see box*).

Medical trailblazer

Ether was first used as an anesthetic in the Bulfinch Pavilion and Ether Dome. In the domed operating theater, illuminated by a skylight, Dr Warren performed the first surgery under general anesthetic on October 16 1846, with ether administered by William Thomas Green Morton. When the patient declared he had felt no pain, Dr Warren said to his colleagues, in a typical Bostonian understatement: 'Gentlemen, this is no humbug.'

Beacon Hill street scene

4: The Waterfront

Map
on page
50

From its earliest days Boston was a busy seaport; in fact until the second half of the 19th century it was the busiest port in the nation. It was said that 15 vessels entered and left the harbor every day of the year. Cargoes included goods for Native Americans on the Pacific coast, who traded sea otter pelts with the Chinese in return for silk. Tea was dispatched all over the world. Sugar and molasses from Barbados and Jamaica were made into rum, then bartered for slaves in Africa. In the latter half of the 19th century the port went into decline, hastened by the 1878 construction of Atlantic Avenue, which severed the piers from the rest of the city.

However, in the 1960s this part of Boston was revitalized, thanks to the building of City Hall Plaza and the restoration of Quincy Market and Faneuil Hall. Abandoned warehouses were resurrected as high-end condominiums, and offices, restaurants, museums and hotels were built, injecting new energy into this historic seaport.

THE BIG DIG

The continually changing face of the area is set to continue until 2005, the projected completion date of a huge project, called the Big Dig, that will reunite the waterfront and downtown.

The multibillion dollar project is undisputedly the largest public works program in US history, and has prompted comparisons to the digging of the Panama Canal. A dizzying logistical undertaking, the ambitious scheme (which has been underway since 1991) will eventually create a Third Harbor Tunnel from Boston to Logan Airport, and should alleviate traffic congestion on the city's Central Artery.

When completed, the Big Dig will have transformed the current six-lane raised portion of I-93 through downtown to an 8 to 10 lane underground highway. Additional facets of the project include two new bridges, which will span the mouth of the Charles River, a new six-lane interchange

Museum Wharf

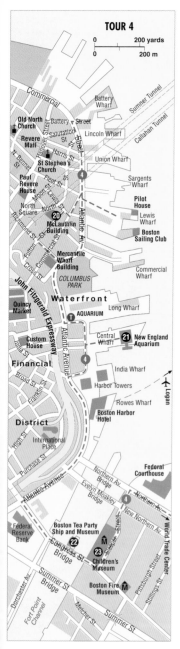

TOUR 4

between I-93 and I-90, and an extension of the Mass Pike (I-90) to Logan Airport via the Ted Williams Tunnel. Until then, erratic traffic patterns, increased noise, heavy machinery, fresh road closings and detours will remain necessary accompaniments to this most ambitious engineering feat.

RECYCLED WAREHOUSES

On heading towards the water from the Quincy-Faneuil Marketplace, the diminutive **Columbus Park** quickly comes into view. Here, the **Rose Kennedy Rose Garden** (named for president JFK's mother) and children's playground are enjoyable places to sit before continuing through the trellised walkway leading to the waterfront.

To the left lies **Commercial Wharf**, which is home to the granite warehouse – now serving as a condominium complex – in which a second set of sails for the *USS Constitution* was made.

Behind you on the far side of Atlantic Avenue, the **Mercantile Wharf Building** is the best example of the area's numerous recycled warehouses. Visitors interested in architecture would do well to continue along Richmond Street, and then turn right on to Fulton Street for a good view of the ★★**McLaughlin Building ⑳**. This five-story 19th-century structure is the first cast-iron building in New England. Each level is separated by a string course, and its perfect repetitive pattern is marred only by the upper level. Turning right on Lewis, head back to Atlantic Avenue, which quickly becomes Commercial Street. Continue northward in the direction of Lincoln Wharf, past **Lewis and Union** wharves.

LEWIS WHARF

At the end of Lewis Wharf stand the **Boston Sailing Club** and a substantial fleet of boats. In 1972, during the renovation of the **Pilot House** located on the north side of this wharf, a false floor was discovered, leading to rumors that the building was being used by opium smugglers, as well as pilots.

More disturbing was the discovery of two entwined skeletons in the basement of **Usher House**, which was demolished in 1880. This fueled speculation that the remains were those of a young sailor and the young wife of an aged man about whom Edgar Allen Poe had written in his 1839 novel, *The Fall of the House of Usher*.

LINCOLN AND LONG WHARVES

Lincoln Wharf's vast five-story red brick building with elegant arched windows has been refurbished into desirable condominiums. Battery Street on the north side of the wharf is where, in 1646, the North Battery was built to control the entrance to the inner harbor and the Charles River. In 1776, British troops were ferried from this point to Charlestown to take their station in the battle of Bunker Hill. Directly beyond this, **Hartt's Naval Yard**, where the *USS Constitution* was built and launched, once stood on the site now occupied by the Coast Guard.

Built in 1710, **Long Wharf** stretches immediately to the south of Columbus Park. It was here,

Map on page 50

Star Attraction
● McLauthlin Building

> **Boston Harborfest**
> Boston has a variety of exciting annual festivals. Among the most popular is the patriotic Boston Harborfest (www.harborfest.com), which takes place during the first week of July in the historic downtown and waterfront areas. Harborfest celebrates Boston's colonial and maritime heritage, as well as the nation's independence.

Columbus Park

in 1790, the *Columbia Rediviva*, the first American ship to sail around the world, moored after her 35-month, nearly 50,000-mile (80,000-km) journey. It was also from this point that in 1895 Joshua Slocum set off in the *Spray* on a solo voyage around the world, lasting 38 months. Boats to Provincetown, the Charlestown Navy Yard, and the Harbor Islands all depart from here. The lovely esplanade at the end of the wharf affords views of North Boston, and of air traffic departing from Logan Airport.

Below: wharfside café
Bottom: the aquarium

CENTRAL WHARF

On the side of Long Wharf lies Central Wharf, which is home to the wonderful ★★ **New England Aquarium** ㉑ (open Mon–Fri 9am–5pm, Sat, Sun and holidays 9am–6pm; admission fee; tel: 973-5200). Once inside, visitors can wind their way past the plucky penguins on the ground floor, and up the ramp that encircles the aquarium's four-story, 200,000-gallon (760,000-liter) ocean tank. The close-up views of sharks, sea turtles, moray eels, and a colorful variety of tropical fish are mesmerizing. The aquarium's café offers traditional New England snacks and lunches, and is child-friendly.

Located in a separate building in the New England Aquarium complex, the new **Simons IMAX**

Theater (toll free tel: 1-866-815-4629) shows daily IMAX and IMAX 3D films of exotic animals and glorious habitats. The aquarium operates **Whale Watch** boat tours to Stellwagen Bank from April-November. Phone 973-5281 for schedules and reservations.

Seafood lovers may enjoy a bite at **Legal Seafoods**, located opposite the aquarium complex, before continuing south past **India Wharf** and onto **Rowes Wharf**, which is entered through a postmodern six-story, gold and russet arch. The Wharf is home to the **Boston Harbor Hotel**, on the site of the 17th-century South Battery, and is the departure point for some harbor cruises.

CONGRESS STREET

On a short wharf in the Channel at Congress Street Bridge stands the **Boston Tea Party Ship and Museum** ㉒, which consists of a small museum and a replica of the *Beaver II*. Unfortunately, a fire in August 2001 forced the closing of the museum, and at the time of writing there is no indication of when it may reopen. Visitors may telephone 338-1773 for updates and information.

Walk beyond the Tea Party Ship and Museum and turn left towards a giant, 40-ft (12-meter) milk bottle, a vestige of a vintage 1930s lunch stand. Here marks the entrance to the **Children's Museum** ㉓ at 300 Congress Street (open daily 10am–5pm, Fri until 9pm; admission fee; tel: 426-8855), a long-standing and popular attraction for kids and grown-ups alike. Visitors are encouraged to touch and manhandle exhibits, to blow bubbles, and to scramble over suspended sculpture.

Upon exiting the museum, turn right towards Northern Avenue. Across the road is **Fan Pier**, an attractive beneficiary of Boston's extensive waterfront restoration and development, and the site of the new **Federal Courthouse**. Continue westward along the avenue to reach the city's **World Trade Center**, and a number of very popular seafood restaurants.

For early risers, there's a daily fish auction at 6.30am around **Pier 4**.

Star Attraction
●New England
Aquarium

👁 **Cultural lessons**
The Kid's Bridge exhibit at the Children's Museum on Congress Street helps children to learn about ethnic diversity and other cultures. A complete two-story Japanese silk merchant's home is a fascinating example of this, while a full-size wigwam and contemporary Native American home show the past lifestyle and present traditions of the region's native people.

Costumed to recall the Boston Tea Party

Map
below

'Make Way for the Ducklings'

5: Back Bay

The botanical bounty of the Public Garden, the elegant brownstones that line Marlborough Street, and the shops, galleries and cafés colorfully strung along Newbury Street, lend this section of Boston a distinctly Parisian air. Baron Haussmann would certainly have recognized kindred spirits in the 19th-century planners who laid out the neat, tree-lined grid of Back Bay. Unlike older areas of the city, where the Puritans' cows are blamed for the idiosyncratic streetscape, Back Bay is orderly and rectangular. Sharp-eyed visitors will even notice that the principal streets running north-south from the Public Garden were named alphabetically, from Arlington to Hereford.

This pretty area was an odorous eyesore a century and a half ago. Boston's original settlement

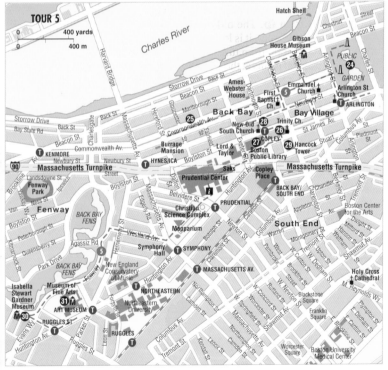

clung to the Shawmut peninsula, a roughly circular clump of hills joined to the mainland by a narrow natural causeway. Tidal marshes of the surrounding Charles River estuary ran up to the back edge of Boston Common, hence the name, 'Back Bay.' In 1813, the Mill Dam was constructed across the Back Bay's northern edge to supply power for mills in South Boston. As a consequence, Back Bay was drained every day, exposing the land to the sun and other elements. Bostonians were also unable to resist the human urge to dump garbage and other waste where they believed no one would notice. But people did take horrified notice; the smell, the putrefaction and the rats couldn't be ignored.

PUBLIC GARDEN

The first improvement began just beyond Boston Common in 1839, with the development of the ★ ★ ★ **Public Garden 24**. The oldest botanical garden in the United States, it is lovingly planted with all manner of flora, from tulips in spring to a selection of tropical palms at the height of summer. In spring and summer, Boston youths pedal the legendary 'swan boats' around the garden's small pond, while resident ducks trail behind in the water seeking food. A picturesque suspension bridge, supposedly the world's shortest, crosses the pond at its center.

Just inside the park's entrance, at the corner of Charles and Beacon streets, are a set of bronze statues depicting the Mallard family of *Make Way for the Ducklings*, Robert McCloskey's classic children's book. Small children adore clambering over the eight ducklings or riding on Mrs Mallard's back. Elsewhere in the park, statues of interest include that of Edward Everett Hale, author of *The Man Without a Country* (at the Charles Street entrance opposite Boston Common), and Charles Sumner, who led abolitionist forces in the US Senate before the Civil War (on the Public Garden's Boylston Street perimeter).

Near the park's Commonwealth Avenue entrance on the Arlington Street perimeter is the

Star Attraction
● Public Garden

Emerald Necklace
Created by architect Frederick Law Olmsted, Boston's excellent park system is a continuous string of nine parks. It includes Boston Common, Public Garden, Commonwealth Avenue Mall, and Back Bay Fens. Further information about Boston's park system can be obtained from the Boston Common Visitor Information Center on Tremont Street, tel: 635-4505.

Swan boats at the Public Garden

Teatime classics

Master classical pianist Oni Buchanan tickles the ivories in the Four Seasons Hotel's elegant Bristol Lounge on Sunday afternoons from 3 to 5pm. Superb music, rarified atmosphere and fine teatime delicacies make Sundays at the Bristol Lounge a good place for classical music lovers to head for (tel: 338-4400).

Ether Monument, commemorating the first use of general anesthesia at Massachusetts General Hospital in 1846.

Facing the Public Garden is the ★★**Bull and Finch Pub**, 84 Beacon Street (tel: 227-9605), the inspiration for *Cheers*, the long-running television sitcom. The interior doesn't resemble the studio set in any way, but that detail doesn't deter the numerous out-of-towners who still flock here several years after the show's 10-year run ended.

STATELY INTERIORS

A heroic statue of General George Washington on horseback faces the 200-ft wide (61-meter) ★★**Commonwealth Avenue Mall** ㉕, first link in the Emerald Necklace chain of green spaces. Imposing Victorian mansions and former hotels line either side of the mall. For a limited view of their grand interiors, step inside the headquarters of the Boston Center for Adult Education, 5 Commonwealth Avenue. The **Ritz-Carlton**, 15 Arlington Street (tel: 536-5700), opened in 1927 as the nation's first Ritz, has a fairly formal lounge with a splendid view of the Public Garden; the same applies to the Bristol Lounge *(see box)* of the **Four Seasons Hotel**, 200 Boylston Street (tel: 338-4400).

Bull and Finch, the Cheers bar

AMBITIOUS PLANNERS

Immediately following the Public Garden's construction, Boston officials focused attention on remaining land in Back Bay as a site for real estate speculation. In 1849, the area was conveniently declared a health hazard and a committee appointed to determine a solution. Fantasy-filled design proposals included an artificial lake, and circus grounds to be built on an artificial island in the Charles River.

In 1857, commissioners approved a development plan that extended Boylston and Beacon streets to the west and created Commonwealth Avenue, as well as Newbury and Marlborough streets. The state organized the removal of land from Pemberton Hill (one of the hills in the original Trimountain, along with Beacon Hill and Mount Vernon), as well as for the hauling of gravel by railroad from Needham. Sale of developable lots would pay for the ambitious public works project.

Star Attractions
● Bull and Finch Pub
● Commonwealth Avenue Mall

BEACON STREET

The Victorian Society of America maintains the 1859 ★ **Gibson House Museum**, 137 Beacon Street (open Wed–Sun; tours at 1pm, 2pm and 3pm; admission fee; tel: 267-6338), one of the first Back Bay mansions built and the only one offering guided tours. The sumptuously furnished dining room is set with a Rockingham service and English Regency chairs. Among the first of Boston's elite to move into Back Bay were John and Isabella ('Belle') Gardner *(see page 62)*, who were married in 1859. At **150 Beacon Street**, they built a mansion on a lot that was a wedding gift from Belle's father.

In 1859, trains up to 35 cars long, each loaded with landfill material, arrived in Back Bay every 45 minutes throughout the day and night. Construction work continued well into the 1880s. Perhaps the musicians playing in Mrs Gardner's Parisian-style drawing room helped to drown out the din of the works.

Below: Commonwealth Avenue Mall
Bottom: lunchtime in the park

DISTINGUISHED ARCHITECTURE

Turn left on Clarendon Street and cross Marlborough Street, one of Back Bay's most attractive residential streets. At the corner of Commonwealth Avenue, the **First Baptist Church**, 110 Commonwealth Avenue (tel: 267-3148) was the first important commission of architect Henry Hobson Richardson. The church's prominent tower is surmounted by a bas-relief of trumpeting angels, sculpted in Paris after Richardson's design by Frédéric-Auguste Bartholdi, who is better known for creating the Statue of Liberty.

Below: Schwarz toy store
Bottom: Newbury Street

Continue south on Clarendon to ★★**Newbury Street**, crowded from Arlington Street to Massachusetts Avenue with art galleries, chic boutiques, restaurants and sidewalk cafés. On Sundays, an orchestra and chorus perform Bach cantatas at ★**Emmanuel Church**, 15 Newbury Street (tel: 536-3356). A distinguished Boston clothier, **Louis Boston**, 234 Berkeley Street (corner of Newbury Street), displays its wares in the former home of the Museum of Natural History, built in 1864, and later succeeded by the Museum of Science. The original site of the Massachusetts Institute of Technology, founded in 1861, stood beside it; the current structure is headquarters of the New England Insurance Company, with historical murals in its lobby.

INVITING THOROUGHFARE

At the south end of Louis Boston is **Boylston Street**, one of the city's busiest thoroughfares of office towers and stores. A huge bronze bear announces the presence of **FAO Schwarz**, the famous toy store, at 440 Boylston Street.

Waterstone's Booksellers, 26 Exeter Street at the corner of Newbury Street (tel: 859-7300), was originally the 'Temple of Working Union of Progressive Spiritualists,' built in 1884, and converted to a theater in 1914.

Backtrack to Dartmouth Street and walk one block south to Copley Square. At the eastern side of Copely Square stands ★★★ **Trinity Church** ㉖, frequently nominated as one of the 10 finest buildings in the United States. Designed by H. H. Richardson in 1872 and completed in 1877, Trinity's French Romanesque form recalls a sybaritic king seated on his throne. The great bulk of the church's granite foundation supports a broad, imposing tower with a simple crown. The building's heavy robes of stone – granite decorated with a ruddy freestone – are richly embroidered with statuary and flecked with the baubles of John LaFarge's stained-glass windows.

Inside, Trinity is a feast of painting and decoration. LaFarge and assistants, including Augustus Saint-Gaudens, achieved the first large-scale frescoes ever attempted in the US. The panels depict a variety of Old and New Testament scenes. LaFarge also designed the majority of Trinity's dazzling stained-glass windows; 'Christ in the Act of Benediction,' a three-paneled window in the west wall of the nave, would be especially inspiring for any minister preaching from the white marble pulpit.

BOSTON PUBLIC LIBRARY

Setting off Trinity's intricate design is the open space of **Copley Square Park**, named for the artist John Singleton Copley (1738–1815), who enjoyed a reputation for the sharpest eye of any painter in the colonies, and counted Samuel Adams and Paul Revere among his clients. Fac-

Star Attractions
● Newbury Street
● Trinity Church

Easy as ABC
The streets that run across Newbury Street from the Public Garden to Massachusetts Avenue are alphabetically arranged. Starting at the Common they are Arlington, Berkeley, Clarendon, Dartmouth, Exeter, Fairfield, Gloucester and Hereford.

Trinity Church

Map on page 54

Below: Boston Public Library
Bottom: Prudential Center

ing Trinity Church on the park's Dartmouth Street perimeter is the original ★★★**Boston Public Library 27**, 666 Boylston Street (open Mon–Thurs 9am–9pm, Fri and Sat 9am–5pm, Sun 1–5pm; tel: 536-5400), designed in the Renaissance Revival style by McKim, Mead and White, and built between 1887 and 1895. It was the first free city library in the country supported by taxes. A 1971 addition by Philip Johnson which fronts Boylston Street is as dignified as the original building, if a little more austere in style.

The old library's sumptuous interior has been extensively renovated, and is home to the **John Singer Sargent Gallery**, which features murals on Judaism and Christianity by the American artist (1856–1925), which some critics rank among his most powerful work. **Bates Hall** is a vast barrel-vaulted reading room swathed in marble, oak and sandstone. The lovely Italian cloistered courtyard in the center of the building allows one to imagine stepping back from modern-day Boston to 16th-century Italy.

NEW OLD SOUTH CHURCH

Completing the architectural triumvirate of Copley Square is ★★**New Old South Church 28**, 645 Boylston Street (so named because the congregation, Boston's third oldest, moved in 1875 to Back Bay from its 1729 home at Old South Meeting House, 310 Washington Street). New Old South's Italian cookie wafer facade in Roxbury puddingstone makes for an exuberant display of the principles of Ruskinian Gothic. Its 246-ft (75-meter) bell-tower was demolished in 1931 because of fears it would topple; the replacement is 15 ft (4½ meters) lower.

JOHN HANCOCK TOWER

Across the street from Trinity on St James Avenue is the 740-ft (225-meter) ★★★**New John Hancock Tower 29**, which had its own architectural problems while under construction in the early 1970s. The dramatic design by I. M. Pei and Partners called for more than 10,000 panes of reflective glass to sheath an irregularly shaped, 60-story tower. Unanticipated stresses, however, caused the window glass to buckle and snap. The 'old' John Hancock Tower, built in 1947, is much-loved for a stylish weather beacon which may be decoded according to a bit of doggerel: 'Steady blue, clear view; flashing blue, clouds due; steady red, rain ahead; flashing red, snow ahead.' (In summer, flashing red indicates the day's Red Sox home game has been cancelled.)

Copley Prudential

If the weather is less than perfect – a not uncommon occurrence – the shopping malls of **Copley Place** and **Prudential Center** ('the Pru' to residents) make a hospitable retreat. Both complexes are somewhat out of character with their surroundings, more suburban than urban. In 1965 when it opened, the 50-story Prudential tower, by Charles Luckman and Associates, heralded a new, modern Boston, but its architectural vision of an antiseptic future quickly dimmed. In the early 1990s, after much public discussion, the cold and windswept complex was enclosed and reincarnated. The transformation was capped, literally and figuratively, in 1995 with a $4 million renovation of the **Top of the Hub** restaurant on

Star Attractions
- **Boston Public Library**
- **New Old South Church**
- **New John Hancock Tower**

Unobserved
Increased concerns about security following the terrorist attacks in September 2001 forced the indefinite closing of the John Hancock Tower's popular rooftop. At present there are no plans to re-open the observation deck to the public. Visitors seeking a comparable aerial view of the city should visit the Prudential Center's Skywalk Observatory *(see main text)*.

Back Bay from the New John Hancock Tower

Map on page 54

the 52nd floor (open Mon–Sat for breakfast, lunch and dinner until 1am; tel: 536-1775). The **Sky-walk Observatory** on the 50th floor (open daily 10am–10pm; tel: 859-0648) gives 360-degree views of the city.. On clear days you can see Cape Cod and the mountains of New Hampshire, 50 miles (80 km) away. The renovation project linked the Pru by glass bridges with neighboring Copley Place, as well as the Hynes Convention Center. More than 100 stores and restaurants as well as three hotels are gathered here.

SCIENCE AND RELIGION

The Pru's exit at Huntington Avenue leads to the ★ **Christian Science Center**, 175 Huntington Avenue (services on Sun at 10am and 7pm, testimonials on Wed at noon and 7.30pm; tel: 450-2000), a sprawling complex that houses the international headquarters of the Church of Christ, Scientist. In 1875, Mary Baker Eddy published *Science and Health with Key to the Scriptures*, in which she outlined her philosophy of Christian Science and sought to restore, as she put it, 'primitive Christianity and its lost element of healing.' While ill herself, Eddy had read a New Testament account of healing by Jesus and was cured. The experience led her to believe that all disease was a product of the mind. Prayer acquired curative powers.

Christian Science Center

In 1892, the Church of Christ, Scientist was formally established in Boston, and the Christian Science Publishing Society began publishing the *Christian Science Monitor* in 1908 – the paper is still going strong today. **The Mother Church** is actually two structures, the first built in 1893–94, and the 'Extension,' with its prominent dome, completed in 1906. Inside the Christian Science Publishing Society Building (1932) is the ★ **Mapparium**, a 30-ft (9-meter) diameter stained-glass globe of the earth bisected by a glass bridge. Around a long reflecting pool are three concrete-faced structures designed by I. M. Pei and Partners and completed in 1973.

ECLECTIC MUSEUM

The ★ ★ ★ **Isabella Stewart Gardner Museum** ㉚, 280 The Fenway (open Tues–Sun 11am–5pm; guided tours Fri at 2.30pm; admission fee; tel: 566-1401), is within easy walking distance of the Museum of Fine Arts; the museum is an eclectic melange of architectural elements, from Venetian window frames to Roman mosaic floor tiles, assembled as a suitably rich setting for galleries crammed with 2,500 objects, most notably masterpieces of European painting by Raphael, Rembrandt and Titian, as well as work by 20th-century masters Degas, Matisse, and James McNeill Whistler. Isabella Stewart Gardner *(see box)* became a serious collector on her father's death in 1891 when she inherited, tax-free, $1.6 million – a sum equivalent to at least $160 million today.

Renowned for her love of flowers, Mrs Gardner directed construction of an interior courtyard with a glass roof so that plants and flowers might thrive year-round. According to provisions in her own will, Fenway Court (the name she gave to her home-cum-museum) was to be preserved exactly as she left it – and so it was until March 1990, when thieves masquerading as police officers removed an estimated $300 million worth of paintings, including *The Concert* by Jan Vermeer, three Rembrandts, five works by Degas and a Manet. To date, they're still missing.

Star Attraction
- Isabella Stewart Gardner Museum

'Mrs Jack'
A native New Yorker of clearly extravagant means, Isabella Stewart married John Lowell Gardner of an equally wealthy Boston family in 1860. Until her death in 1924, 'Mrs Jack' cultivated a reputation for unconventional behavior in the primly conventional society of Victorian Boston. Although she apparently did not keep lions in her cellar or walk them on a leash down Beacon Street (as legend has it), Mrs Gardner had wide-ranging interests, from Oriental philosophy to the Boston Red Sox.

Courtyard of the Isabella Stewart Gardner Museum

Map
on page
54

BSO outdoors
Every July the Boston Symphony Orchestra (BSO) transfers from the Symphony Hall to the Hatch Shell, the outdoor music stand on the banks of the Charles River. Here, they delight large audiences with their Boston Pops Esplanade Concerts for four weeks. Tel: 266-1200 for more information and tickets.

OPENING NIGHT

Fenway Court was opened for the first time on New Year's Night 1903 with a concert by members of the Boston Symphony Orchestra; Mrs Gardner engaged many private performances by Paderewski, Nellie Melba and Gerald and Sarah Murphy, who serenaded her with African-American folk songs. The Gardner Museum continues to present more than 125 concerts a year.

THE BEST ART

The ★★★ **Museum of Fine Arts** ③ (MFA), 465 Huntington Avenue (open Mon–Tues 10am–4.45pm, Wed–Fri 10am–9.45pm; admission fee; tel: 267-9300) has departments in Asiatic art, Egyptian art, classical art, European decorative arts and sculpture, American decorative arts and sculpture, paintings, drawings and photographs, textiles and costumes, and modern art. Together, the MFA's holdings make it one of the nation's most outstanding art museums. In addition, it regularly stages critically-acclaimed 'super shows.'

On the lawn in front of the entrance to the original 1909 museum building by Guy Lowell is the MFA's trademark sculpture by Cyrus Dallin, *Appeal to the Great Spirit*, depicting a Plains Indian in feathered headdress with arms outstretched and eyes uplifted.

The museum's bunker-like West Wing (the entrance is at Museum Road), was designed by I. M. Pei, and since its opening in 1981 is where most special exhibitions are hung.

The MFA's massive collection has something to please everyone, and any abbreviated guide will necessarily ignore numerous equally worthwhile selections. Nevertheless, visitors will want to seek out several highlights.

Museum of Fine Arts

LOCAL MASTERS

Boston's premier colonial portrait artist, John Singleton Copley (1738–1815), is represented by dozens of excellent pieces, notably life-like portraits of the patriots Samuel Adams and Paul

Revere. The latter's own exquisite work in silver is well-represented in the museum. Major New England artists frequently depicted local subjects, and among such works are *Boston Harbor* by Fitz Hugh Lane, *Fog Warning* by Winslow Homer, and *Boston Common at Twilight* by Frederick Childe Hassam.

One of the largest collections anywhere of art from Japan and China, the Asiatic Department spans from Chinese ceramics of the 6th century to 18th-century Japanese scrolls depicting *The Gay Quarters of Kyoto*. These were chiefly amassed in the 19th century by local collectors while on trade voyages to the Far East in clipper ships.

The Egyptian rooms have mummies, statues, jewelry and funereal objects dating to the Old Kingdom (2778– 2360 BCE). A 'pair statue' depicting King Mycerinus and Queen Kha-Merer-Nebty is the oldest known of its kind.

FRENCH COLLECTION

Throughout the 19th century, Boston collectors gravitated to works by French painters and were among the first anywhere to adopt the Impressionists. Major works by Degas, Delacroix, Gauguin, Millet, Monet, Manet, Pissaro and Renoir are among the most popular.

Star Attraction
● **Museum of Fine Arts**

Below: exhibit at the Museum of Fine Arts (bottom)

Map on page 68

Innovative art
The Copley Society of Boston, America's oldest non-profit art association, is home to some innovative shows that are reason enough to venture to Newbury Street. 158 Newbury Street, tel: 536-5049. Open Tues–Sat 10.30am–5.30pm.

6: Harvard Square

On October 25, 1636, the same day it passed legislation forbidding the sale of lace for garments except for 'binding or small edging lace,' the Massachusetts General Court also 'agreed to give £400 towards a schoale or colledge' to be established at Newtowne on the north bank of the Charles River, 5 miles (8 km) from Boston.

The Puritans' commitment to higher education in their fledgling settlement was hardly trifling, since £400 represented almost one-quarter of the Massachusetts Bay Colony's total tax levy that year. When you consider that the endowment of Harvard University today easily exceeds $6 billion, it's clear that the return on the Puritans' original investment reckoned in the advancement of learning is incalculable.

HISTORIC LEGACY

Harvard Square

In September 1638, shortly after the college was opened, a 30-year-old clergyman of a well-to-do London family succumbed to consumption in Charlestown. On his deathbed, the Rev. John Harvard declared his wish to leave half his estate (about £1,700) and all his library to the college; the next spring, the General Court resolved to name the school in his honor as well as to change the name of Newtowne to Cambridge, after the English city where many of the Puritan leaders had been educated.

TAKE THE 'T'

Because parking is so limited around Harvard Square, the easiest way to get there is via the MBTA (also known as the 'T') Red Line to Harvard station. Escalators and stairs emerge from underground onto the center stage of Harvard Square, where Massachusetts Avenue, JFK Drive, and Brattle Street merge. An information kiosk operated by **Cambridge Tourism Office** (tel: 441-2884) provides maps and brochures and is located at the head of the stairs. Beside the 'T' station entrance is **Out of Town News** (tel: 354-7777), with a wide collection of national and international newspapers and magazines. The **Harvard Cooperative Society**, known familiarly as 'the Coop' (pronounced like chicken coop) stands across the street at 1400 Massachusetts Avenue (tel: 499-2000), and has a full line of souvenirs and clothing emblazoned with the Harvard University crest.

Star Attraction
● John Harvard statue

THE STATUE OF THREE LIES

Johnston Gate, the main entrance to **Harvard Yard**, is 100 yards (91 meters) west on Massachusetts Avenue from the 'T' station. **Massachusetts Hall** (1720), to the right, is the oldest surviving college building and houses the office of the college president. To the left, **Harvard Hall** is the third structure of that name, built in 1764 after a fire consumed what was then the largest library in America, including books bequeathed by John Harvard.

Designed by Charles Bulfinch in 1813, the granite-faced **University Hall** lies across the lawn of the Old Yard, behind the 1884 ★ ★ ★ **statue of John Harvard**, by Daniel Chester French. It is known whimsically as 'the statue of three lies' because (1) the figure is not John Harvard – no likeness of him is known to exist – but Sherman Hoar, a member of the Class of 1882; (2) John

Below: al fresco studies
Bottom: John Harvard statue

Map below

Harvard did not found the college, but was its first important benefactor; and (3) the college was established not in 1638, the year of Harvard's death, but two years earlier.

Black art

Born in 1845 to a Chippewa mother and a free black father, Edmonia Lewis was America's first black woman sculptor. After moving to Boston in 1863, she specialized in sculpting representations of abolitionists and civil war heroes. Lewis' marble sculpture of the poet Henry Wadsworth Longfellow can be seen on the second floor of Harvard University's Fogg Museum at 32 Quincy Street in Cambridge (tel: 495-9400, www.artmuseums.harvard.edu).

MEMORIAL CHURCH

Continuing further in Harvard Yard, the Tercentary Quadrangle, or so-called New Yard beyond University Hall, is the site of the school's annual commencement activities. The white steeple of **Memorial Church**, built in 1931 to honor Harvard students and alumni killed in World War I, should look familiar – the model was the spire of Old North Church.

The quadrangle's most dominant structure is the 12-columned portico of the ★★★**Widener Memorial Library** ②, named for Harry Elkins Widener, a member of the Class of 1907 who went down with the *Titanic* in 1912. Harvard's vast

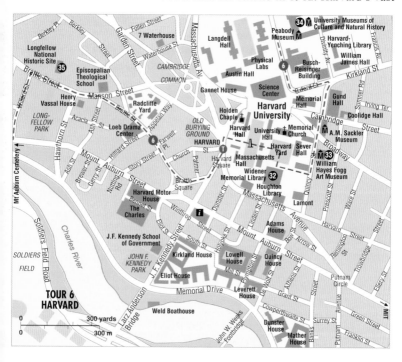

TOUR 6
HARVARD

| 0 | 300 yards |
| 0 | 300 m |

book collection – exceeded in the US only by the Library of Congress and the New York Public Library – includes a 1623 First Folio of Shakespeare's plays, as well as a Gutenberg bible, which are displayed in the **Widener Memorial Room**. In the adjacent **Houghton Library**, a display of rare books includes the only surviving volume from John Harvard's library.

HARVARD AND THE ARTS

Follow a footpath at the bottom of the Widener Library stairs roughly east to Quincy Street. Immediately striking by its stark appearance is the **Carpenter Center for the Visual Arts** (1961), 24 Quincy Street, the only US building by Le Corbusier. In a basement theater of the austere concrete structure, the **Harvard Film Archive** (tel: 495-4700) presents films from around the world.

Below: exhibit at the Fogg Art Museum (bottom)

The ★★**Fogg Art Museum** ㉝, 32 Quincy Street (open Mon–Sat 10am–5pm, Sun 1–5pm; admission fee – no charge Wed all day and Sat 10am–noon; tel: 495-9400), is the oldest of Harvard's nine museums. It opened in 1895 and covers American and European painting and sculpture as well as housing temporary exhibitions. The Fogg's current home was completed in 1927; a handsome replica of an Italian loggia lies behind an unassuming neo-Georgian facade. A single Harvard art museums admission also allows entrance to the galleries of Central and Northern European art in the **Busch-Reisinger Museum** (tel: 495-9400), which may be entered through the Fogg, as well as the nearby **Arthur M. Sackler Museum**, 485 Broadway (tel: 495-9400), which has Classical works as well as Chinese, Japanese and Islamic art.

HISTORICAL GEMS

Turn right on Quincy Street and again cross Cambridge Street. On the left is **Memorial Hall**, begun in 1870 to honor Harvard's Civil War dead; its auditorium, Sanders Theater, hosts lectures and

Map
on page
68

Native museum
The Peabody Museum of Archaeology and Ethnology's outstanding Hall of the North American Indian (Intersection of Quincy Street and Broadway, Cambridge, tel: 495-9400) focuses on the interaction between Native American and European newcomers through thematic displays and artifacts.

music concerts. To the right is the library and studios of **Graham Gund Hall** (1969), home of the Graduate School of Design. Turn right at Kirkland Street, then left on Oxford Street, leading to the sprawling complex, on the right, of the ★★**Harvard University Museums of Natural History ㉞** (open daily 9am–5pm; admission fee – no charge Wed 3–5pm; tel: 495-3045).

Of the 100,000-plus works of art in the various museums, the **Ware Collection of Glass Flowers,** on the third floor of the ★★★**Botanical Museum,** is the most popular. Other highlights include Native American cultural artifacts at the **Peabody Museum of Archaeology and Ethnology**; the world's largest-known turtle shell in the **Museum of Comparative Zoology**; meteorites and a 3,040-carat topaz gem in the **Mineralogical and Geological Museum**; and photography from the Middle East in the **Semitic Museum**.

BRATTLE STREET

Return to the Harvard Square 'T' station and cross to Brattle Street. The Cambridge Center for Adult Education has its headquarters in the **William Brattle House**, 42 Brattle Street, built in 1727 by the town's wealthiest citizen. Longfellow's poem *The Village Blacksmith* honored Dexter Pratt, his neighbor and the original owner of 56 Brattle

Radcliffe Yard

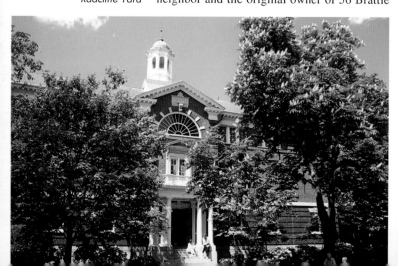

Street, constructed in 1808 and now the **Hi-Rise Pie Co.** (tel: 492-3003). The 'spreading chestnut' mentioned in *The Village Blacksmith* was cut down in 1876, despite protests from Longfellow himself. The **Loeb Drama Center**, 64 Brattle Street, performs classic and contemporary works by the American Repertory Theater throughout the year. **Radcliffe Yard**, of the women's college of the same name, lies opposite.

At the corner of Ash Street, the **Stoughton House**, 90 Brattle Street (not open to the public), was built in 1883 by Henry Hobson Richardson, architect of Copley Square's Trinity Church, and ranks as one of the first and most successful examples of the Shingle Style (the house was renovated and enlarged in 1900 by Richardson's successor firm).

Star Attractions
● **Harvard University Museums of Natural History**
● **Botanical Museum**
● **Longfellow National Historic Site**

HIAWATHA'S CREATOR

Henry Wadsworth Longfellow, creator of Evangline and Hiawatha and myth-maker of Paul Revere's ride, lived at 105 Brattle Street from 1837 until his death in 1882. ★★★**Longfellow National Historic Site ⑳** (tel: 876-4491) preserves the belongings and the memory not only of Longfellow, but also of another famous resident, General George Washington, who made his headquarters here in 1775 and 1776 after taking command of the Continental Army. In the study, for example, are both the Chippendale chair where Washington sat while forming strategy with his staff, and a folding desk where Longfellow wrote. An elaborate flower garden at the estate was begun by Longfellow in 1845. Across the street, **Longfellow Park** includes a memorial sculpture by Daniel Chester French and the home Longfellow built for his son in 1870.

Longfellow House

DISTINGUISHED RESTING PLACE

Leaving Longfellow Park, continue on Brattle Street a short distance to Willard Street, turn left toward the Charles River, then right on Mt Auburn Street. A 15-minute walk, crossing busy

Map on page 68

Route 2, leads to ★★ **Mt Auburn Cemetery**, the nation's first garden cemetery, which opened in 1831 (the graveyard may be more easily and quickly reached by a 'trackless trolley' bus from Harvard Square station, route 71).

Final resting place of Longfellow, Bulfinch, Winslow Homer, Mary Baker Eddy, and many other distinguished Massachusetts natives, Mt Auburn Cemetery may be appreciated for the ornate architecture of its tombs as well as for the splendor of its plantings. The calm of this urban oasis attracts a wide range of migratory birds.

Below: Mt Auburn Cemetery
Bottom: Rogers Building, MIT

MIT

Return again to Harvard Square. At an MBTA bus stop on Massachusetts Avenue, in front of the yellow-clapboard **Wadsworth House** (General Washington's headquarters before he moved to 105 Brattle Street), take the route no. 1 bus (marked, 'Dudley') about 1½ miles (2.5 km) along Massachusetts Avenue to the **Massachusetts Institute of Technology**. Founded in Boston in 1861, MIT moved from Copley Square to the banks of the Charles River in Cambridge in 1916. Scientists working at the school's Servomechanisms Lab developed 'Whirlwind,' the grandfather of digital computers; when completed in 1951, it filled several large rooms.

TOURING THE CAMPUSES

On the East Campus, the large, impressive granite-domed ★★**Rogers Building**, 77 Massachusetts Avenue, is known to MIT students as 'Lobby 7.' An MIT information office inside (tel: 253-4795) offers free maps and guided campus tours. The bare lobby is representative of the entire labyrinthine complex, linked by long, factory-like corridors. Immediately accessible from the Rogers Building (named for geologist William Barton Rogers, 1804–82, the school's founder and first president) is the **Francis Russell Hart Nautical Museum**, which has detailed displays of ships' models, and the **Margaret Hutchinson Compton Gallery**, exhibiting items from the MIT historical collection.

Directly across from the main entrance to Lobby 7, follow what students call for obvious reasons 'the infinite corridor', through several buildings, to an exit onto Killian Court, where Henry Moore's rotund masterpiece, *Three-Piece Reclining Figure, Draped* (1973) is surrounded by the trim, classical forms of the Maclaurin Buildings. Maclaurin, a Scott, was president of MIT when he moved it from Boston to Cambridge. **Hayden Memorial Library**, 160 Memorial Drive, displays art and sculpture.

FINNISH STYLE

Across Massachusetts Avenue on MIT's West Campus, **Kresge Auditorium** (rear of 48 Massachusetts Avenue) is the most prominent feature. A carapace of glass and steel, with a wood-paneled auditorium seating 1,238, Kresge was designed in 1954 by the Finnish architect Eero Saarinen, who is also responsible for the brick cylinder of the nearby windowless **MIT Chapel**.

A half-mile (1 km) from the center of MIT's campus is the **MIT Museum**, 265 Massachusetts Avenue (tel: 253-4444), featuring scientific instruments and documents on the school's history. The **MIT List Visual Art Center**, 20 Ames Street (tel: 253-4680), devoted to contemporary art in all media, is on the East Campus.

Star Attractions
- Mt Auburn Cemetery
- Rogers Building

Prize winners
More than half of MIT's 10,000 students are enrolled in graduate programs, and more than 30 of its faculty have won Nobel Prizes. It was here that the World Wide Web and the magnetic core memory that made digital computers possible were developed.

Kresge Auditorium

Map on pages 76–7

Below: Memorial Day procession, Concord
Bottom: Munroe Tavern

Excursion 1

Lexington and Concord

On Saturday, April 17, 1775, Paul Revere and others in Boston observed an alarming trend in British troop movements. Redcoats of the 29th Regiment had been stationed at the Common since 1768, and they were watched closely by resident patriots. Unexpectedly, routine patrols were cancelled and work was begun to ready troop boats for action. Bostonians surmised that the British were preparing either to arrest John Hancock and Samuel Adams, who were in Lexington for a meeting of the Massachusetts Provincial Congress, or else to seize a cache of arms hidden in nearby Concord. Revere, principal rider for the Boston Committee of Safety, rode out the next morning to warn them, then returned to Boston. He would make the same journey again that night – with momentous effect.

STANDING THEIR GROUND

The clash of British troops and Massachusetts 'Minutemen' on April 19, 1775, pitted Goliath against David – with a similar result. First on the Lexington Green, then at the North Bridge across the Concord River, the pressure cooker that were the 13 colonies boiled over. In Lexington, Captain Parker told his men: 'Stand your ground, don't fire unless fired upon, but if they mean to have a war, let it begin here!' And so it did. By day's end, after nearly 40 miles of marching, the Redcoats returned to Boston, leaving a bloody chain of dead and wounded on both sides.

WHERE THE WAR BEGAN

Lexington, 12 miles (19 km) west of Boston, is reached by Massachusetts Avenue from Cambridge or from Route 2. MBTA buses go to Lexington Center from the Alewife Red Line station, and MBTA commuter rail trains stop in Concord on the Fitchburg line from North Station, as well as the Red Line's Porter Square Station. At the junction of Massachusetts Avenue (Route 2A), just outside historic Lexington, is the ★ **Museum of Our National Heritage**, 33 Marrett Road, Lexington (tel: 781-861-6559). Founded in 1976 as a Bicentennial gift by the Scottish Rite of Freemasonry, the museum presents changing exhibits on American history and popular culture. *Lexington Alarm'd*, is a permanent show about the opening of the American Revolutionary War.

While the owner and his family hid in nearby woods, British Redcoats arriving from Boston made a temporary HQ on April 19, 1775 at the **Munroe Tavern**, 1332 Massachusetts Avenue (tel: 781-674-9238). As they retreated later in the day, the Redcoats left their wounded here.

A mile farther on Massachusetts Avenue is ★★**Battle Green,** the country's most famous 2-acre plot. The **Minuteman Statue**, by Henry Hudson Kitson, depicting a Yankee farmer with musket, commemorates the heroes of the day. The town's helpful **Visitors Center**, run by the Lexington Chamber of Commerce, is at 1875 Massachusetts Avenue (tel: 781-862-1450).

Star Attraction
● Battle Green

Sculpture garden
A popular venue for contemporary art, the DeCordova Museum and Sculpture Park (51 Sandy Pond Road, Lincoln, tel: 781-259-8355) encompasses lakeside vistas, intriguing exhibitions, and a 35-acre (14-hectare) sculpture garden.

BUCKMAN TAVERN

When the Minutemen assembled at dawn, they were not sure how to greet the British. Several

Buckman Tavern

Map below

of those under command of Captain John Parker hadn't even bothered to bring ammunition. No one knows who fired the first shot. At colorful battle recreations held here on the third Monday of April, gunfire commences simultaneously.

Wounded Minutemen were carried inside ★**Buckman Tavern**, One Bedford Street (tel: 781-862-5598), on the east side of Battle Green. By the door are holes where wayward Redcoat musket balls struck. Inside is the tavern's original 17th-century furniture and cooking equipment. Altogether, eight Massachusetts men were killed and 10 wounded. Struck by a musket ball, Captain Parker was finished off with a Redcoat bayonet thrust. The Americans had fired in a disorderly manner, and only one British soldier received a flesh wound.

Literary trail
One way of unravelling the literature and history of Boston is through the guided tours of homes, haunts, and landscapes of some of America's most cherished literary giants. The Literary Trail threads through Boston, Cambridge, and Concord (tel: 350-0358, www.littrail.org).

FEISTY PATRIOTS

A short stroll up Hancock Street leads to the **Hancock-Clarke House**, 36 Hancock Street (tel: 781-861-0928). When unsuspecting Redcoats released Paul Revere shortly after his famous ride, he scurried here to warn fellow patriots Samuel Adams

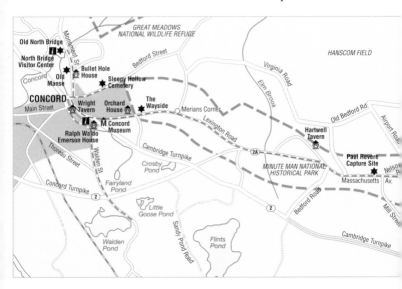

and John Hancock. Revere was able to see the pair off before British troops arrived at Lexington Green for the fateful confrontation with the Minutemen. As they sped away in a carriage heading in the opposite direction, the feisty Adams remarked about the glorious morning. Hancock, a well-to-do dandy, thought his companion referred to the weather. 'I mean,' said Adams patiently, 'what a glorious morning for America.'

Star Attraction
● Battle Road
Visitors Center

ROUTE 2A

Traveling west on Route 2A, you can trace what is left of the **Battle Road**, along which the confident British marched toward Concord to the music of fife and drum. The 750-acre (303-hectare) **Minute Man National Historic Park** is on the left. One mile from Lexington on the right is the ★★★**Battle Road Visitors Center**, off Route 2A (tel: 781-862-7753), considered the best place for historical information.

Arranged in a row on the right of Route 2A (Lexington Road) are three historic houses associated with 19th-century Concord, when the New England village was a kind of Athens in

Below: Battle Road Visitors Center
Bottom: Battle Road

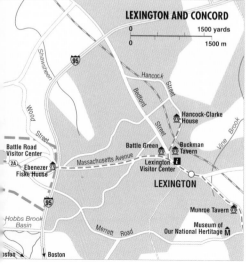

LEXINGTON AND CONCORD

Map on pages 76–7

miniature, a literary and philosophical hotbed. Here Ralph Waldo Emerson, the Transcendentalist philosopher, composed his essays and provided occasional meals to his friend and neighbor, Henry David Thoreau, when he was living at Walden Pond.

Also residing in Concord were the novelist Nathaniel Hawthorne, the poet William Ellery Channing, and the education reformer and famous father Amos Bronson Alcott. At ★★**Orchard House**, 399 Lexington Road (tel: 978-369-4118), the Alcott family lived from 1858 to 1877, and here Louisa May Alcott wrote *Little Women*. At **The Wayside**, 455 Lexington Road (tel: 978-369-6975), Nathaniel Hawthorne lived from 1852 until his death in 1864. Next door, the **Grapevine Cottage**, 491 Lexington Road (not open to the public), displays a plaque that details how, in 1843, Ephraim Wales Bull first sowed the Concord grape at his nearby farm.

Below: The Wayside.
Bottom: Orchard House

STATELY HOMESTEADS

At the junction of Route 2A and the Cambridge Turnpike, the ★★**Concord Museum**, 200 Lexington Road (open Jan–Mar: Mon–Sat 11am–4pm; Sun 1–4pm; Apr–Dec: Mon–Sat 9am–5pm; Sun noon–5pm; tel: 978-369-9763) has 17 rooms of antiques, including a lantern purported to have

hung beside another in Old North Church as a signal to Paul Revere. Because of fear of fire, Emerson's Study was transferred here from the nearby wooden Emerson House. In the Thoreau Room is the bed where the back-to-nature essayist slept at Walden Pond; the museum boasts the world's largest collection of Thoreau artifacts. Across the road, **Ralph Waldo Emerson House**, 28 Cambridge Turnpike, on Route 2A (tel: 978-369-2236) has books from his library as well as the writer's own furnishings.

CONCORD CENTER

A 15-minute walk reaches the center of Concord, whose Chamber of Commerce has a **tourist information center** at Heywood Street, (tel: 978-369-3120). **Monument Square** has a memorial to those who died in the Civil War. The **Colonial Inn**, 48 Monument Square (tel: 978-369-9200) serves hearty meals, as it has done since before the Revolution. The town has many attractive boutiques as well as the generously stocked **Concord Bookshop** at 65 Main Street.

Concord's prominent permanent population resides at ★★**Sleepy Hollow Cemetery**, a short stroll from the Inn along Bedford Street. In the northeast corner, at **Author's Ridge**, rest the Alcotts (Louisa May and her father, who died two days apart in 1888, shared the same birthday and the same funeral), along with Hawthorne, Thoreau and Emerson. A bronze tablet on Emerson's quartz stone grave marker declares: 'The passive master lent his hand/To the vast soul o'er which him planned.' Less lofty are the sentiments engraved over Ephraim Wales Bull's final resting place – 'He sowed, others reaped' (the developer of the Concord grape had failed to profit from his work).

REDCOATS AND MINUTEMEN

Return to Monument Square and once again, pick up the trail of Redcoats and Minuteman along Monument Street, passing the **Old Manse** (tel:

Star Attractions
- ● Orchard House
- ● Concord Museum
- ● Sleepy Hollow Cemetery

Natural poet
A native of Concord and the third child of a pencil maker, Henry David Thoreau graduated from Harvard in 1837 and turned his attention to teaching — without true satisfaction. Under the guidance of Ralph Waldo Emerson who relocated to Concord, he discovered that his true calling was that of poet and philosopher.

The Colonial Inn

Map
on pages
76–7

978-369-3909), built in 1770 for the Rev. William Emerson, and later occupied by Ralph Waldo Emerson and Nathaniel Hawthorne. Enter the ★★★ **National Historic Park**, and cross a contemporary reconstruction of the famous 'rude bridge.' On the other side of Old North Bridge waits the Minuteman statue by Concord resident Daniel Chester French. Further information can be found at **North Bridge Visitor Center**, 174 Liberty Street (tel: 978-369-6993).

At North Bridge, Major John Pitcairn and his men crossed the Concord River to take control of the house of Colonel James Barrett, where American arms were supposedly stockpiled. When fire began in the town courthouse and elsewhere, Concord's defenders let fly with 'the shot heard round the world.' The element of surprise was in the Massachusetts men's favor, and the Redcoats took their first serious casualties. In short order, the British began a disorderly retreat to Boston.

Below: National Historic Park
Bottom: Walden Pond

WALDEN POND

In summer, the crowd of bathers at the glacial ★★★ **Walden Pond** (tel: 978-369-3254), a 10-minute walk from the intersection of Routes 2 and 126, overwhelms any search for the quiet solitude that Thoreau sought here. A cairn of stones marks the site where, from 1845 to 1847, young Henry David Thoreau lived in a one-room cabin which he built on Emerson's estate. Thoreau recounted his experience of his time on the pond in *Walden, or Life in the Woods* (1854), and there declared his intention plainly: 'I went to the woods because I wished to live deliberately, to front only the essential facts of life, and see if I could not learn what it had to teach, and not, when I came to die, discover that I had not lived.'

Conservationists have battled tirelessly to protect this area from commercial development. Thanks to the good work of the Walden Woods Project, nearly 90 acres (36 hectares) of the 333 acres (135 hectares) surrounding Walden Pond Reservation have been preserved.

Excursion 2

Salem

Curiously for a city that's a by-word for hysterical intolerance, Salem takes its name from *shalom*, the Hebrew word for 'peace.' Today, of course, Salem is an attractive and richly historical waterfront city 20 miles (32 km) north of Boston, and is decidedly peaceful. At its defining moment in 1692, however, the air here and in surrounding settlements was charged with fear and recrimination. In January that year, several young women, including the daughter and niece of minister Samuel Parris, began to exhibit strange and inexplicable behavior at their home in Salem Village (now called Danvers). Their symptoms included blasphemous screaming, convulsive seizures, trance-like states and mysterious 'spells.'

THE FAMOUS WITCH-HUNT

Pressed to identify the source of their torments, the girls denounced Tituba, a slave in the Parris household who was born in Barbados, and who may have told the girls provocative Caribbean tales; they also blamed two local women, Sarah Osborne, a widow of some property who enjoyed male company and did not regularly attend church

Map on page 82

Star Attractions
- **National Historic Park**
- **Walden Pond**

Below: the witch village with (bottom) a gruesome museum exhibit

services, and the destitute Sarah Good. Tituba's 'confession' – she claimed to have conversed with winged cats and red rats – persuaded officials that demonic possession was rife in their midst. In the ensuing 'witch-hunt' 27 townspeople were convicted, 19 were hanged and four died in jail. The tide finally turned when a Boston merchant complained to Governor William Phips, who dissolved the special court session in October.

An astonishing maritime legacy also draws visitors. Following the Revolutionary War, Salem thrived in the new China Trade and became one of the world's busiest ports, if only briefly. When they had the opportunity, Salem's canny captains cornered the world market on black pepper, tea, spices and silk. The wealth they made was used in Salem to build fabulous mansions.

Cotton Mather
Throughout 1646 the Rev. Cotton Mather, a leading Boston pastor, never missed an execution in Salem. He was a roaring orator at all hangings, galloping his horse to the front of the crowd of onlookers and leaping from his saddle on to the gallows platform. There he would rant and rave, preach and pray, berating and denouncing the victim about to die.

PEDESTRIAN TOUR

Salem's attractions make for an active and rewarding day trip, and its compact area make it possible to tour almost entirely by foot. It is easily reached on the MBTA Rockport commuter rail

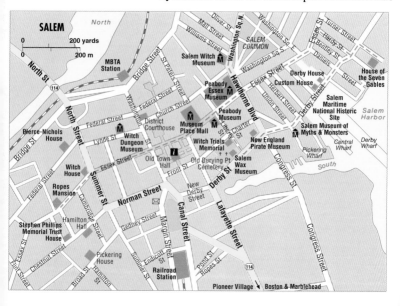

line from North Station. A self-guided **Heritage Trail** snakes through the city for around 2 miles (3 km) and connects all major sites. **National Park Service Visitor Center**, 2 Liberty Street (tel: 978-740-1650) provides maps and information as well as presenting films and exhibits. **Salem Trolley Corp.** (tel: 978-744 5469) departs from here regularly for over a dozen attractions.

Everyone's first stop in 'the Witch City' is naturally the ★★★ **Witch Museum**, Washington Square (tel: 978-744-1692). Inside the turreted Romanesque castle are 13 stage sets with life-size models plus a gripping audio-visual presentation.

Surrounding the Visitor Center, in a multibuilding complex, is the ★★★ **Peabody Essex Museum**, East India Square, Salem (open Apr–Oct: Mon–Sat 10am–5pm, Sun noon–5pm; Nov–Mar: closed Mon; admission fee; tel: 978-745-9500). The Peabody Museum of Salem, founded in 1799 by mariners and merchants of the East India Marine Society, is the nation's oldest continuously operating museum; in 1992, it merged with the Essex Institute, a historical society founded in 1821. The combined collections feature nearly half a million objects in 30 galleries of permanent and changing exhibitions.

Below: an unpleasant exhibit at the (bottom) Witch Museum

MONUMENT TO TOLERANCE

One block south on Liberty Street at the corner of Charter Street is the ★ **Witch Trials Memorial**. Dedicated in 1992, the trial's tricentennial, the design inspires reflection on human rights and tolerance. Behind is the **Old Burying Point**, Salem's oldest burying ground (1637).

At the corner of Charter Street and Derby Street is the **Salem Wax Museum**, 288 Derby Street (tel: 978-740-2929), which opened in 1993.

Directly opposite is ★★ **Salem Witch Village**, 282 Rear Derby Street (tel: 978-740-9229), where you can learn about witchcraft through the ages.

Before they became obsessed with witches, Salem's merchants hired Captain Kidd in 1691 to hunt down the hated Blackbeard. When he failed to capture the scourge of New England's high

Map on page 82

Below: Salem Wharf
Bottom: House of the
Seven Gables

seas, Kidd turned to piracy himself. Swashbuck-ling stories are told at the **New England Pirate Museum**, 274 Derby Street (open May–Oct: Mon–Fri 10am–5pm; tel: 978-741-2800).

Continuing eastward on Derby Street brings you to ★ **Pickering Wharf** (tel: 978-745-9540), a harborside marketplace of boutiques and restaurants. Directly adjacent is the ★★★ **Salem Maritime National Historic Site**, 174 Derby Street (tel: 978-740-1680). Guided tours cover maritime buildings of the 9-acre (3.5-hectare) Derby Wharf and the nearby 1819 ★ **Custom House**, where Nathaniel Hawthorne worked.

EDWARDIAN TOURS

Return to Derby Street, continue east and turn right at Hardy Street. By the harbor's edge lies the ★★★ **House of the Seven Gables**, 54 Turner Street (open Nov–June: daily 10am–5pm except Jan; July–Oct daily 10am–7pm; admission fee; tel: 978-744-0991). Guides in Edwardian costume welcome visitors to this 1668 mansion, which supposedly inspired Hawthorne's romantic novel; you can also visit the novelist's birthplace nearby and other 17th-century dwellings.

Pick up the Heritage Trail again at the corner of Hardy and Essex streets and stroll west to the ★★ **Witch House**, 310 Essex Street (tel: 978-744-0180). The restored home of witch trial Judge Jonathan Corwin, this is the only structure still standing with direct ties to the 1692 events.

Salem's ★★★ **Chestnut Street**, a National Historic Landmark, has a superb collection of Federal era townhouses. The Peabody Essex Museum maintains three fine houses in the area, including the ★ **Ropes Mansion** on Essex Street.

In Forest River Park, at the junction of Route 1A and Route 129, is ★ **Salem 1630: Pioneer Village** (tel: 978-745-0525), a re-created 17th-century New England fishing village. The 5-acre (2-hectare) site includes wigwams, thatched roof cottages, animals grazing in a meadow, and a blacksmith at work. The site, about 3 miles (5 km) from Salem's center, is accessible by bus.

Excursion 3

Cape Ann – Gloucester – Rockport – Essex

Of all areas in Massachusetts settled by English colonists, only Plymouth has a longer history than Cape Ann. In 1623, the Dorchester Company under Roger Conant established a fishing post at what is now Gloucester. The first hardy English fishermen have long since been supplanted by equally hardy Italians and Portuguese. Sadly, overfishing of the once plentiful stock of cod and ground fish has endangered their livelihood. Its commercial link with the sea may be loosening, but Cape Ann has not lost hold of those seeking contact with the water, found at the end of a pier lined with restaurants and art galleries.

TO THE SEA

En route to Gloucester on Route 127, visitors pass through the town's well-to-do Magnolia section. An imposing presence set above rocky shores, the ★**Hammond Castle Museum**, 80 Hesperus Avenue (open Sat and Sun 10–3; admission fee; tel: 978-283-2080), was a showcase for inventor John Hays Hammond Jr's eclectic collection of European art objects. A 'reanimation' shows slices of life from Romanesque, Medieval and

Map on page 86

Star Attractions
- Maritime National Historic Site
- House of the Seven Gables
- Witch House
- Chestnut Street

Trails and tours
Cape Ann Chamber of Commerce, 33 Commercial Street (tel: 978-283-1601/1-800-321-0133) provides maps and information, including a map and guide to the Gloucester Maritime Trail, four self-guided walking tours. Otherwise, Moby Dick (tel: 978-281-3825) gives tours, by means of amphibious vehicles, around town and in the ocean from late May to early September.

Gloucester

Map below

Schooner festival

Every Labor Day weekend (nearest to May 1), schooners of all sizes meet in Gloucester to race at the annual Gloucester Schooner Festival. Festival events include a parade of sails, fireworks, and a lighted boat parade. For more information on this and other events, visit the Gloucester Tourism Commission's website at www.gloucesterma.com or call toll free on 1-800-649-6839.

Renaissance Italy, France and Spain; the central courtyard opens onto a mini-town square with 15th-century French house facades.

In 1623, Gloucester's first settlers arrived at Fishermen's Field, near what is now **Betty Smith Park** and **Stage Fort Park**, overlooking Gloucester Harbor on Stacy Boulevard, near the fisherman's statue. **The Gloucester Visitors' Welcoming Center** is also at the site.

The ★★★ '**Man at the Wheel**,' depicting a wind-lashed sailor and inscribed to 'They that Go down to the Sea in Ships,' stands as a gateway to Gloucester on Stacy Boulevard (Route 127). The trademark sculpture was commissioned in 1923 and created locally by Leonard Craske.

DOWNTOWN

The Downtown Loop, a 1-mile (1.5-km) walking trail, begins at **St Peter's Park**, named for the patron saint of fishermen. Turn right at the Harbor Loop, and continue past the US Coast Guard Station, a working military base, closed to the public. In summer, the ★★**Schooner** *Adventure* (tel: 978-281-8079), a National Historic Landmark, is docked not far away (open to visitors in summer on Saturday and Sunday; *Adventure*'s winter berth is at Jodrey State Fish Pier). Built of oak and pine in nearby Essex, the 121-ft (37- meter) schooner spent around 27 years fishing the North Atlantic's rich outer banks from Gloucester and Boston.

Cross through a parking lot and climb a set of stairs beside the Police Station to Main Street, turn left, then right to Pleasant Street. ★★★**Cape Ann Historical Museum**, Cape Ann Historical Association, 27 Pleasant Street, at the corner of Federal Street, (open Tues–Sat 10am–5pm; admission fee; tel: 978-283-0455) exhibits the nation's largest collection of paintings and drawings by Fitz Hugh Lane (1804–65), one of America's most important 19th-century artists. The museum's Fisheries Maritime Galleries feature three historically significant vessels, including *Centennial*, the vessel Alfred Johnson used in the first single-handed crossing of the Atlantic.

Retrace Pleasant Street to Middle Street, which is lined with attractive late 18th-century homes. A 15-room Georgian mansion, the **Sargent-Murray-Gilman-Hough House**, 49 Middle Street (tel: 978-281-2432), is worth a tour. At the corner of Middle Street and Church Street, the **Universalist Church**, erected in 1805, was the first of its kind in the US and houses a Paul Revere bell.

EAST GLOUCESTER

In East Gloucester, the **North Shore Art Association**, 197 East Main Street (open Mon–Sat 10am–5pm; Sun noon–5pm; tel: 978-283-1857) founded in 1923, is the oldest art association of its kind in the US. A large collection of paintings and sculpture is on show in a renovated wharf building overlooking Smith Cove. Turn right toward the water along Rocky Neck Avenue, home to a number of art galleries and restaurants. Still more galleries and artists' studios are open at the ★★**Rocky Neck Art Colony**, which is the oldest continuously operating art colony in the country, and is full of charm and ambiance.

Continuing toward Eastern Point, ★★★**Beauport, The Sleeper-McCann House**, 75 Eastern

Star Attractions
- 'Man at the Wheel'
- Schooner Adventure
- Cape Ann Historical Museum
- Rocky Neck Art Colony
- Beauport

Below: Schooner Adventure
Bottom: Rocky Neck Art Colony

Map on page 86

Map on page 86

Point Blvd. (tel: 978-283-0800) overlooks Gloucester Harbor from the east. In 1907 Henry Davis Sleeper, a prominent collector and interior designer, began the house's construction, which evolved over nearly 30 years into a maze of 40 rooms filled with vast collections of American and European objects, all artfully arranged by Sleeper. Charles and Helena McCann bought Beauport after Sleeper's death and installed their own extensive collection of Chinese export porcelain, but otherwise preserved the house intact.

WHALE WATCHING

The self-proclaimed ★★★ **'Whale-Watching Capital of the World,'** Gloucester benefits from its proximity to the well-known fisheries haunt, the Stellwagen Banks (as a result, whale-watching trips taken from Gloucester last half as long as those leaving from Boston).

EASTERN POINT LIGHTHOUSE

Established in 1832, Gloucester's Eastern Point Lighthouse is located on the outer edge of Gloucester Harbor. Home to master painter Winslow Homer in 1880, this Gothic wooden lighthouse is still operational and is managed by the US Coastguard.

Whale of a time
Local operators for whale watching trips include: Cape Ann Whale Watch and the Whale Conservation Institute, Rose's Wharf (tel: 978-283-5110/1-800-877-5110); Capt. Bill & Sons and the Cetacean Research Unit, Harbor Loop (tel: 978-283-6995/1-800-339-4253); Yankee Whale Watch and the Atlantic Cetacean Research Center, 75W Essex Avenue – Route 133 (tel: 978-283-0313/1-800-942-5464); Seven Seas Whale Watch, Seven Seas Wharf, Rogers Street (tel: 978-283-1776/1-800-238-1776).

Whale watching in the bay

SCENIC ROCKPORT

At the tip of Cape Ann, **Rockport** ranks among America's most picturesque harbor towns. ★★★**Motif #1**, on Bradley wharf, is a quaint clapboard sail loft decorated with buoys that is supposedly the most photographed and most painted building in the country. Bearskin Neck, a finger of land curling around the harbor and lined with shops and restaurants, ends at **Old Stone Fort**, a small stockade built by public subscription during the War of 1812.

Like Gloucester, Rockport has long served as an inspiring setting for artists enamored of the sea. ★★**Rockport Art Association**, 12 Main Street (open June–Columbus Day ie. 2nd Mon in Oct: Mon–Sat 10am–5pm; Sun noon–5pm; Feb–May and day after Columbus Day–Dec 24: Tues–Fri 10am–4pm, Sat 10am–5pm and Sun noon–5pm; tel: 978-546-6604), has a fine exhibition of paintings, graphics and sculptures by local artists. In 1814, the British man-of-war *Nymph* fired at the **Old Sloop Congregational Church**, Main Street, to silence its bell, which had been rung to alarm the town. The shot landed in the tower support, however, where it can still be seen.

Star Attractions
● Whale watching
● Motif #1
● Rockport Art Association
● Paper House

Below: seafood specialties
Bottom: coast near Rockford

CHARMING ODDITIES

At the opposite end of town is the **Hannah Jumper House** (corner of Mount Pleasant Street and Atlantic Avenue), whose namesake led the women of Rockport in the Hatchet Gang Raid, July 8, 1856, to rid the town of liquor. Rockport is still 'dry'. A rocky mount at the end of Atlantic Avenue, the **Headlands** offers spectacular views of the harbor, and attracts artists and picnickers.

Rockport's oddest attraction is the ★★**Paper House** on Pigeon Hill Street, Pigeon Cove. Swedish immigrant Ellis Stenman, who read nine newspapers daily, fashioned his unique abode between 1922 and 1942 from 100,000 newspapers; the walls are made of 215 layers of newspaper, rolled, glued and varnished. Unusual

Map on page 86

furnishings include a grandfather clock made from newspapers of the capital cities of the then 48 states, and a writing desk made from stories about Charles Lindbergh's trans-Atlantic flight.

Fried clams start here
One hot July day in 1916, Lawrence Woodman tossed some clams into a pan of boiling oil and created the heavenly dish of fried clams. Woodman's Lobster Pool, Main Street, Route 133, (tel: 978-768-6057) is still serving up its original owner's invention, to the delight of its many customers.

ESSEX

A rural town of 3,000 that was settled in 1634, **Essex** is famed for its long tradition of ship-building and clamming. The town is located on the northern flank of Cape Ann, and is a major antique center, with dozens of shops located within a stone's throw of one another. An after-noon of sightseeing or boating on the Essex River can be sweetened by a fresh meal of seafood at any of a dozen restaurants arranged along a scenic coastal stretch of Route 133.

As fishing is to Gloucester, shipbuilding was to Essex, where over the years 4,000 vessels were built, most of them in the 19th century. ★★ **Essex Shipbuilding Museum** on John Wise Avenue, (open Thurs–Sun noon–5pm; admission fee; tel: 978-768-7541) features drawings, tools, pho-tographs, rigged ship models and other sailing paraphernalia, displayed in an 1834 schoolhouse.

The highlight of the **Essex Clamfest**, the town's annual tribute to the magnificent mussel, held on the second Saturday in September, is a clam chowder tasting competition.

Antique store in Essex

Excursion 4

Harbor Islands

Map on page 92

In November of 1996, following 24 years as a designated state park, the 30 Boston Harbor Islands were added to the National Park System by the Federal Government, and henceforth became known as the **Boston Harbor Islands National Recreation Area**.

The Boston Harbor Islands played an important role in Boston's cultural and economic history. Native Americans used to use them as hunting and burial grounds, colonial settlers farmed them, and later they served as battlegrounds and internment camps. Since their recognition as a National Park, the islands have enjoyed a renaissance, as the region seeks to rebuild its historical and ecological ties to Massachusetts Bay. Although much of the islands' future is yet to be defined, six are the focal point of visitor activity: Georges, Peddocks, Grape, Bumpkin, Lovells and Gallops.

Star Attraction
● Essex Shipbuilding Museum

SUMMER HUNTING GROUND

A true refuge for mainland deer, and prized summer hunting ground for Native Americans hundreds of years ago, today **Deer Island** is a peninsula linked to the town of **Winthrop**, and site of the Massachusetts Water Resources Authority Deer Island sewage treatment plant. Deer Island's massive sludge treatment project and once controversial 10-mile (16 km) sewage outlet pipe that carries outflow far from Boston Harbor (added to the island in the late 1990s) have had a tremendously positive impact on the health of harbor wildlife: harbor porpoises have returned and the health of edible fish has improved.

Located 10 miles (16 km) from downtown Boston, the rocky formation of **Graves** is the farthest harbor island, while the 214-acre (87-hectare) **Long Island** is the biggest. Long Island is linked by bridge to **Moon Island**, **Quincy**, and the **South Shore**.

Boston Light on Little Brewster

Map below

Barren lands
There is no drinking water on the islands, so bring ample water as well as any food you may need. George Island has the only refreshment stand. All the islands have toilet facilities.

GEORGES ISLAND

George's Island is the island gateway to the other harbor island, and offers visitors recreational fishing along its shores, and a slice of the harbor's military history through **Fort Warren**. Built in 1833, the fort served as a training ground for Confederate soldiers in the Civil War, and as a prison for their captives.

A 45-minute 7-mile (11 km) boat ride from downtown Boston, the island has a refreshment stand, picnic areas, guided tours, and splendid views of the city's skyline, Boston Light *(see next page)*, and nearby **Gallop's** and **Lovell's** islands. Ferryboats run from George's to Gallop's, Lovell's, Peddock's, Grape and Bumpkin Islands from June to October, with a weekend service in the spring and fall.

Lovell's Island offers special permits for overnight camping near the ruins of **Fort Standish**, built in 1900. During World War II, nearby Gallop's Island was the site of a US Maritime Training School and a hospital, as evidenced by the remains of large drumlin, which dominate it.

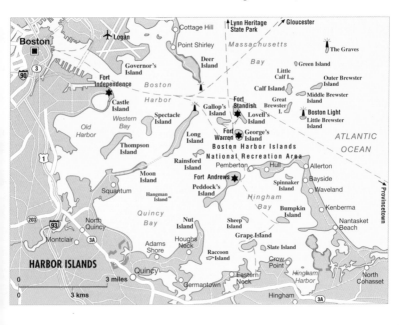

HARBOR ISLANDS

PEDDOCK'S ISLAND

Just over a mile (1½ km) to the south lies the third largest harbor island. **Peddock's Island**. where 4,100-year-old-bones were discovered in what was the oldest archeological find in New England. The island is home to a marsh, a brackish pond, many walking trails, and the remains of **Fort Andrews**, which was built around the time of the Spanish American War and housed prisoners during World War II.

GRAPE AND BUMPKIN

Grape and **Bumpkin** islands are reachable by ferryboats that run daily in the spring and summer. Both are located in Hingham Bay and are sheltered by the long arm of Nantasket Beach and the town of Hull. Grape Island is one of the most lovely of the islands, offering a myriad of trails and bountiful wildlife, including skunks, rabbits, and a plethora of birds. Bumpkin is home to the remains of a children's hospital, and a farmhouse that has been overtaken with indigenous vegetation, including bayberries and wild raspberries. For information, schedules and permits for camping on Bumpkin or other Harbor Islands, telephone 223-8666.

   Great Brewster offers unique panoramas of the inner harbor, the Atlantic, and Little Brewster's charming ★★ **Boston Light**. The lighthouse was erected in 1716, and was the first one in the nation, but it was blown up by the departing British in 1776. The current structure was built in 1782 and is a National Historic Landmark. It remains the only lighthouse in the country that is still manned by keepers.

   Other harbor islands can be reached by private boat, or by tours led by organizations such as the **Friends of Boston Harbor** and the **New England Aquarium**. Both groups lead annual lighthouse visits to Little Brewster's Boston Light. Friends of Boston Harbor ferry visitors to **Thompson Island**, which is owned and managed by the private, non-profit Thompson Island Outward Bound Education Center.

Star Attraction
● Boston Light

Georges Island

Architecture

Contributing to Boston's atmosphere as a 'European city' is its well-preserved collection of architectural styles dating to the late 17th century. On the Freedom Trail, the Paul Revere House, built of wood in 1680 in a simple style, is the city's oldest structure; the equestrian/patriot lived there from 1770 until 1800.

America's first trained architect, Charles Bulfinch, toured Europe from 1785 to 1787 at the suggestion of Thomas Jefferson, and was especially impressed by Georgian London. On his return to Boston, Bulfinch, barely 24, boldly submitted a plan for a new Massachusetts State House. His likely inspiration was London's Somerset House. Over the next few decades, Bulfinch designed important residences for many wealthy Boston families, and completed drawings for the new Massachusetts General Hospital in 1816, before leaving for Washington, DC, and an assignment as architect of the US Capitol.

When Boston began filling in the Back Bay in 1857, the work sparked one of the city's most prolonged periods of real estate development. Today, the vast area between Boylston Street and Beacon Street, from the Public Garden to Massachusetts Avenue, is virtually an open-air museum of 19th-century residential architecture, predominantly brownstone townhouses. Boston's greatest architect of the period, Henry Hobson Richardson, was a Louisiana native who came to Harvard in 1855 as a student and remained in the area until 1876. Richardson's masterpiece is the Romanesque styled Trinity Church at Copley Square, with stained-glass windows by Louis Tiffany and frescoes by John LaFarge.

Boston's built environment is superbly complemented by the Emerald Necklace. Designed by Frederick Law Olmsted, who also created the plans for New York City's Central Park, the Emerald Necklace was begun in 1881. The chain of thickets and open glades, brackish marshlands and freshwater ponds, wild forests and manicured flower beds stretches 5 miles (8 km) from the

Spoken word
The Brookline Booksmith is an independent bookstore which hosts an ongoing series of readings by writers at its location at 279 Harvard Street in Brookline. Visit their website at www.brooklinebooksmith.com for complete information about upcoming readers, or call them on 566-6660.

Left: the prow of the USS Constitution
Below: 17th-century vernacular, Munroe Tavern

urban confines of Boston Common to the open country of Franklin Park.

In the first half of the 20th century, Boston's economic ills meant that much was preserved that might otherwise have been destroyed. Efforts in the late 1950s at so-called 'urban renewal' obliterated the West End and Scollay Square, replacing narrow streets and quaint structures with I.M. Pei's vast, barren plaza of Government Center. A new City Hall (1968) in the stark brutalist style of Kallman, McKinnell & Knowles is disdained by both critics and citizens.

The skyline was further shaped by I.M. Pei with the John Hancock Tower (1976), New England's tallest building. The International Style's other great practitioner, Philip Johnson, has contributed several buildings, most notably his addition to the Boston Public Library (1972).

Literature

The first American printer in the English language was Stephen Day (or Daye) who published *The Bay Psalm Book,* a literal translation of Biblical psalms from the Hebrew, in Boston in 1640. In 1663, John Eliot, the 'Apostle to the Indians,' published a complete edition of the Old and New Testaments translated into the Algonquin tongue spoken by Massachusetts natives; it was the first Bible published in North America.

Early Puritan laws requiring the elementary education of all children were intended so that a congregation might read scriptures. Reading and writing, however, quickly became a means of self-expression and, by the 1830s, Boston was hailed as the 'Athens of America.' Led by Ralph Waldo Emerson of Concord, local intellectuals nurtured the development of Transcendentalism, which indelibly shaped an emerging American social philosophy. One of the nation's first feminists, Margaret Fuller, was editor of *The Dial*, an influential literary journal that published work by Emerson, Henry David Thoreau and others. In Salem, Nathaniel Hawthorne completed *The Scarlett Letter* in 1850 and *The House of Seven*

Below: John Hancock Tower
Bottom: Nathaniel Hawthorne

Gables in 1851. *Walden*, Thoreau's musings on the simple life he led in a cabin at Walden Pond, Concord, appeared in 1854; it took the author five years to sell the 2,000 copies printed. Louisa May Alcott, another Concord resident who was raised with Emerson, Thoreau and Fuller as regular family guests, published Part I of *Little Women* in 1868. The best known account of the Salem witchcraft trials is Arthur Miller's *The Crucible*.

Theater and Music

For its range of cultural venues, Boston has few equals in the United States. Over time, Boston's stages, concert halls and music clubs have nurtured artists of the highest caliber.

The Boston Symphony Orchestra under the direction of Seiji Ozawa is a longstanding critical and popular success.

The Pulitzer Prize-winning playwright August Wilson regularly brings his dramas of African-American life to the Huntington Theatre before taking them on to Broadway. At the American Repertory Theatre, the Tony-winning actress Cherry Jones was for many years a company member.

The choreographer Mark Morris cultivated his talents at the Dance Umbrella and still returns regularly to Boston.

Blue Man Group
Three blue men make music, splash paint, and examine chaos theory in a high-energy show that is truly one of a kind, and earned them a Drama Desk Award. Charles Playhouse, 74 Warrenton Street, 426-6912 for info, 931-ARTS for tickets.

Below: the Globe Corner Bookstore
Bottom: street jazzers

CLASSICAL MUSIC

Boston Lyric Opera, 45 Franklin Street (tel: 542-4912) stages three productions annually. **Boston Symphony Orchestra**, Symphony Hall, 301 Massachusetts Avenue (tel: 266-1492) performs October–April. It moves to Tanglewood (in Lenox) for the summer, making way for the **Boston Pops** to play light musical fare from mid-May through mid-July (in addition to performances at Symphony Hall, the Boston Pops play a series of free concerts, most notably a Fourth of July extravaganza complete with fireworks, at the Hatch Shell on the Charles River Esplanade).

Boston Philharmonic performs at Jordan Hall, 30 Gainsborough Street (tel: 868-6696).

Handel & Haydn Society, 300 Massachusetts Avenue (tel: 266-3605), has played Handel's *Messiah* annually since 1854. **Longy School of Music**, One Follen Street, Cambridge (tel: 876-0956) has an active concert schedule year-round.

New England Conservatory of Music, 30 Gainsborough Street (tel: 262-1120) presents lectures, seminars and several hundred free concerts each year at Jordan Hall.

DANCE

Ballet Theatre of Boston, 186 Massachusetts Avenue (tel: 262-0961), brings contemporary works to the Emerson Majestic Theatre. **Boston Ballet**, 19 Clarendon Street (tel: 695-6950), presents a glittery *Nutcracker* at Christmas, as well as a variety of classical and contemporary programs at the Wang Center. **Dance Umbrella**, 515 Washington Street (tel: 482-7570), also stages its productions at the Emerson Majestic Theatre and has earned a national reputation.

Concert goers

THEATERS & DRAMA COMPANIES

American Repertory Theatre, 64 Brattle Street, Cambridge (tel: 495-2668) shows original plays and restaged classics. **Colonial Theatre**, 106 Boylston Street (tel: 426-9366) presents major Broadway shows. **Emerson Majestic Theatre**,

219 Tremont Street (tel: 824-8000) has been restored by its new owners, Emerson College.

Huntington Theatre Company, 264 Huntington Avenue (tel: 266-0800), stages both classic and contemporary plays September–June. **Lyric Stage**, 140 Clarendon Street (tel: 437-7172), produces new plays and classics including the perennial favorite *A Child's Christmas in Wales*.

At the **Charles Playhouse**, 74 Warrenton Street (tel: 426-5225), *Shear Madness*, a comedy whodunit with local references, is America's longest-running play.

Schubert Theatre, 265 Tremont Street (tel: 482-9393), is a prominent venue for Broadway try-outs. **Wang Center for the Performing Arts**, 270 Tremont Street (tel: 482-9393), is an elegantly restored movie palace, and is now home to major theatre, music and dance performances.

Wheelock Family Theatre, Wheelock College, 180 The Riverway (tel: 734-5203), caters for a young audience.

First Night

Boston's popular **First Night** celebrations offer more than 250 family-oriented events, including opera, theater, classical music, ethnic music and dance. Visit the First Night website at www.firstnight.org or call 617-536-4100.

Music at the Hatch Shell

FOOD AND DRINK

In the home of the bean and the cod, don't expect to find much of either. Boston baked beans long ago joined chicken à la king as endangered American food species. Cod that once were thick enough in the ocean waters off the Massachusetts coast to be caught in baskets have all but disappeared from over-fishing. Likewise, a New England boiled dinner of corned beef and cabbage is a rarity served only on St Patrick's Day.

The contemporary selection of fresh seafood available in most restaurants includes monkfish, red snapper and Arctic char, among others. What hasn't changed is that a visit to Boston still isn't complete without a bowl of steaming clam chowder and a boiled lobster. Otherwise, the culinary possibilities are virtually endless, from pasta to pad thai, burgers to burritos, and steak to sushi.

Has-beans

Boston is thought of as the land of the home of the bean chowder, traditionally cooked in molasses and sugar. But you will have to search a score of restaurants before finding a menu that offers a side order of Boston brick-oven baked beans.

Massachusetts does, however, provide staples for the traditional Thanksgiving meal (on the fourth Thursday in November) with Cape Cod cranberry sauce and New England squash. Another local tradition is *The Boston Cooking School Cookbook*, written by a graduate, Fanny Farmer, in 1889. A stickler for accurate quantities, she was known as "the mother of level measurements".

During the 1990s, a microbrewing revolution began to sweep America. It started in Boston and appropriately was sparked by Samuel Adams, 'patriot-brewer.' Today, ales and lagers with the 'Sam Adams' label are ubiquitous at city restaurants and bars. A half dozen 'brew pubs' scattered around Boston and Cambridge offer up a variety of fresh beer on tap to help wash down generous plates of hearty pub grub.

Restaurants

The restaurants listed are divided into three categories. $$$: expensive ($25 or more per person); $$: moderate ($15-25 per person); $: inexpensive (under $15 per person). Prices do not include wine, tax, and gratuities (it's customary to tip 15% of the total bill). Whatever the night or season, reservations are recommended, although not all restaurants will accept them, particularly on weekends.

Ambrosia, 116 Huntington Ave. (tel: 247-2400). Anthony Ambrose juxtaposes Asian spices with native seafood and calls on his travels in France and his work experience there with Japanese chefs. $$$

Aujourd'hui, Four Seasons Hotel, 200 Boylston Street (tel: 338-4400). Formal atmosphere for fine continental and creative American cuisine. Elegant setting near Public Garden. $$$

Biba, 272 Boylston Street (tel: 426-7878). Lydia Shire's showcase for contemporary cuisine. $$$

Bob The Chef's, 604 Columbus Avenue (tel: 536-6204). Serving up Cajun dishes like jambalaya, crab cakes, and fried catfish. The Sunday Jazz and Gospel brunches are a must for music lovers. $

Brew Moon, 115 Stuart Street/City Place (tel: 523-6467). A casual, contemporary atmosphere, with on-site microbrewery and American cuisine. $$

Café Intrigue, Boston Harbor Hotel, 70 Rowes Wharf on Atlantic Avenue (tel: 439-3995). Casual harborside blend of regional and native cuisine. $

Chau Chau City, 83 Essex Street (tel: 350-7777). This large Chinatown restaurant specializes in seafood, and dim sum, which is very popular. Free parking after 6pm. $

Daily Catch, 323 Hanover Street (tel: 523-8567). Fresh fish are the specialty here, as the name suggests. $$

Dom's, 10 Bartlett Street (tel: 367-8979). A North End landmark, memorable for Italian owner Dominic Caposella's habit of sitting with patrons as they order. $$

Durgin-Park, Faneuil Hall Marketplace, North Market (tel: 227-2038). A landmark. Try scrod (young cod or haddock) and chowder. $

Dynasty, 33 Edinboro Street (tel: 350-7777). Chinatown's most popular dim sum served early on Sunday. $

Fugakyu Japanese Restaurant, 1280 Beacon Street, Brookline (tel: 739-0000). Serving excellent Japanese food and sushi. Adventurous diners can opt to handpick their meals direct from live fish tanks. Open for lunch, dinner, and late-night dining. $$$

Hamersley's Bistro, 533 Tremont Street (tel: 423-2700). Contemporary American food influenced by French country cuisine. Masterful; upscale decor. $$$

Lala Rokh, 97 Mt. Vernon Street, Beacon Hill (tel: 720-5511). Delightful Persian restaurant whose menu includes scrumptious Armenian, Indian and Turkish dishes. $$

Legal Seafoods, Long Wharf, 255 State Street, (Tel: 227-3115). Serving ultra fresh seafood at this and other locations around Boston, including the Prudential Center, Copley Place, and Park Square. $$

Locke-Ober, 3 Winter Place (tel: 542-1340). Established in 1875 and still serving American classics such as Oysters Rockefeller, Lobster Savan-

> **Ice is nice**
> Americans eat more ice cream than any other nation, and New Englanders consume 14 pints (6½ liters) more annually than the next most ice-cream hungry state. Bostonians can be obsessive about their ice cream, which they eat with 'jimmies' — sprinkles on the top.

nah, and Indian pudding. Jacket and tie required. $$$

Maison Robert, 45 School Street (tel: 227-3370). Elegant formal dining room serving French and American cuisine; summer outdoor terrace. $$$

Mantra, 83 Main Street, Charlestown (tel: 242-6009). Gourmet French-Indian food in a lavish setting. Upscale dress code required. $$$

Morton's of Chicago, One Exeter Plaza (tel: 266-5858). Prime dry-aged beef and chops, fresh seafood. Extensive wine list. $$$.

Oak Room Steakhouse, 138 St. James Avenue (tel: 267-5300). Elegant dining in a stately venue. $$$

Olive's, 10 City Square, Charlestown (tel: 242-1999). Excellent Italian restaurant. Reservations only for parties of 6 or more; smaller parties should be prepared to wait. $$$

La Piccola Venezia, 263 Hanover Street (tel: 523-3888). Large portions; no-frills and inexpensive too. $

Pignoli, 79 Park Square (tel: 338-7500). Wide-ranging selection of creatively-prepared Italian dishes. $$$

Pizzeria Regina, 11½ Thatcher Street (tel: 227-0765). Delicious pizzas in the great atmosphere of the North End,

Seasons Restaurant, Bostonian Hotel at Faneuil Hall Marketplace (tel: 523-3600). Inventive American cuisine served in an enclosed rooftop setting overlooking the marketplace. $$$

Sol Azteca, 73 Union Street, Newton Center (tel: 964-0920). Fine Mexican food in a pleasant atmosphere. Their sangria is a must. $–$$

Turner Fisheries Bar & Restaurant, 10 Huntington Avenue (tel: 424-7425). In Westin Hotel. Try the delicious oysters. $$$

Ye Olde Union Oyster House, 41 Union Street (tel: 227-2750). America's oldest restaurant, established 1826, serving traditional New England seafood. *(See page 30.)* $$

Zaftics, 335 Harvard Street, Brookline, 02446 (tel: 975-0075). Traditional Jewish cuisine, including Borscht, saurkraut, and potato pancakes. Good value. $

Cambridge

Asmara, 739 Massachusetts Avenue, Cambridge (tel: 864-7447). Small, comfortable and attractive restaurant serving delicious Ethiopian food. $

Bombay Club, 57 JFK Street (tel: 661-8100). Indian lunch buffets and authentic à la carte too. $$

Cambridge Common, 1667 Massachusetts Avenue, Cambridge (tel: 547-1228). Traditional American favorites in a lively atmosphere. $

Casablanca, 40 Brattle Street (tel: 876-0999). Moroccan dishes and American burgers. $

Green Street Grill, 280 Green Street, Cambridge (tel: 876-1655). Colorful, comfortable and informal restaurant. Menu highlights include cod and conch fritters and pan seared Chilean sea bass. $–$$

Grendel's Den, 89 Winthrop Street (tel: 491-1160). With working fireplace in winter. $

The Helmand, 143 1st Street, Cambridge (tel: 492-4646). A terrific Afghan restaurant, serving traditional cuisine such as kebabs and lovely rice dishes. Good selection of vegetarian dishes. Open for dinner only. $$–$$$

John Harvard Brew House, 33 Dunster Street (tel: 868-3585). Restaurant-cum-brewery, in Cambridge since 1637. Offering great food and beer. $$

Rialto, Charles Hotel, One Bennett Street (tel: 661-5050). Regional cuisine with flair. $$$

Salamander, One Atheneum Street (tel: 225-2121). Wood grille dishes unusually prepared with an Asian accent. $$$

An outdoor café and student haunt in Harvard Square

SHOPPING

In the Victorian era, 'proper Bostonians' were notorious for thrift, disregard for fashion, and general lack of acquisitiveness. Their ranks have since thinned considerably, however, and today one can feel free to spend liberally while shopping throughout the Boston area, and satisfy just about any taste, cosmopolitan and otherwise. There is no certainly no lack of souvenirs for visitors wanting to bring a bit of Boston home.

Downtown Crossing (Washington Street)

When Edward Filene opened **Filene's Automatic Bargain Basement** in 1909, fellow merchants wondered if he'd lost his mind. Any item on the shelves that didn't sell immediately was discounted over several weeks until it was either sold or given away. Filene's Basement was not profitable for 10 years, but it has done rather well ever since. For special sales 'in the basement,' eager shoppers gather long before doors open. **Filene's**, a traditional department store, is located on several floors above.

Shop the net

The best thing about shopping in a foreign town is simply walking the streets and malls, and seeing what catches your eye in the windows. Newbury Street and Faneuil Hall Marketplace are tops from this point of view. But anybody with rather more dedicated shopping plans could try logging on to websites such as shopping.boston.com or boston.citysearch.com before they start out. Here you can search for stores by product, name and neighborhood, and you can also find out where to get 'soaked, rubbed and refreshed' at the city's spas.

Across a pedestrian-only section of Summer Street, **Macy's** (formerly Jordan Marsh) is the competition. It's a quick hop from Macy's to the **Brattle Book Shop**, 9 West Street, the nation's oldest bookseller, which sells rare and used books. In the immediate area are numerous jewelers, and a number of pushcarts featuring tourist-oriented crafts and trinkets.

Faneuil Hall Marketplace/ Marketplace Center

In three restored buildings from the 19th-century, **North Market, South Market** and the colonnaded **Quincy Market**, and **Marketplace Center**, an adjacent modern retail/office tower, can be found just about everything to eat, drink, wear or read at more than 150 specialty shops and 22 diverse restaurants. Before the area was re-created as a 'festival marketplace' in the mid-1970s, it had served as a center of merchant activity for a century and a half *(see also page 27)*.

Over time, the Faneuil Hall Marketplace has come to resemble an ordinary shopping mall within an extraordinary historic setting. Shops include Waterstone's, the Disney Store, and the Celtic Weaver, specializing in handmade Irish sweaters and clothing. **Bull Market** pushcarts showcase the original and colorful wares of over 100 New England artisans and entrepreneurs.

Newbury Street

'Rodeo Drive East' stretches from Arlington Street at the Ritz Carlton to the **Tower Records** building at Massachusetts Avenue. From wealthy international students to grungy aspiring rock stars, Newbury Street affords some of the best people-watching in

Boston, and plenty of pleasant sidewalk cafés encourage the sport. As one walks west, the shops gradually shift from chic (**Giorgio Armani Boutique**, 22 Newbury Street) to cheap (**Mystery Train Records**, 306 Newbury Street, which has a wide selection of 'recycled' music).

The city's **art galleries** congregate here, as well as the **Society of Arts & Crafts**, 175 Newbury Street, which sells jewelry and furniture crafted by local artisans. **Gargoyles, Grotesques & Chimeras**, 262 Newbury Street, sells artfully-rendered reproduction statues for something a bit different, and **Allston Beat**, 348 Newbury Street, is a clothing store favored by the city's alternative crowd. The café at **Sonsie Restaurant**, 327 Newbury, aspires to Parisian sophistication, while across the street, **Trident Bookseller & Cafe**, 338 Newbury Street, caters to New Age interests.

Copley Place/Shops at Prudential Center

You can shop till you drop and never worry about the raindrops in this sprawling indoor mall complex near Copley Square. Walkways connect to various buildings, including the Hynes Convention Center. **Neiman Marcus** and **Saks Fifth Avenue** department stores are among more than 100 merchants and food purveyors.

Cambridge

HMV Records and the Gap might be found almost anywhere, but in the intellectual hothouse of **Harvard Square**, their neighbors include **Schoenhof's Foreign Books**, 76A Mt Auburn Street, the area's finest international bookseller, and the **Cambridge Artists Cooperative**, 59A Church Street, which sells jewelry, clothing, pottery and crafts made by local artisans.

For Harvard College souvenirs, the **Harvard Cooperative Society** (known locally as 'the Coop'), 1400 Massachusetts Avenue, has a wide selection of branded sweatshirts, caps, T-shirts and ties.

For mall-hoppers, the **Shops at Charles Place** (adjacent to the Charles Hotel) and the **Cambridge-side Galleria** near the Museum of Science have the usual assortment of department and specialty stores.

ANTIQUES

If proper Bostonians weren't terribly enamored of fashion, they were decidedly fond of outfitting their homes with fine furniture and artworks. What hasn't been passed down through the generations frequently ends up in local antique shops. **Boston Antique Co-op**, 119 Charles Street (tel: 227-9810), is one of many such specialty stores in the Beacon Hill area.

You'll find a number of upscale shops all along Charles Street. An increasing number are also opening in the South End.

MUSEUM SHOPS

Many of Boston's fine museums, such as Isabella Gardner Stewart Museum (2 Palace Road, *see page 62*), have a variety of unique and attractive wares. Located on lively Central Wharf, the **New England Aquarium Gift Shop** sells gifts and treasures related to all things aquatic.

The **Museum of Fine Arts**, Boston, Bookstore and Shop (465 Huntington Avenue), offers beautiful jewelry, stationery and vases as well as a stunning collection of silk scarves, while the **Museum of Science Gift Shop** (1 Science Park, Cambridge) provides junior scientists with all the gear necessary to launch experiments and scientific explorations at home.

NIGHTLIFE

The rap for visitors is that the city of Boston is a daylight-hours only attraction. After you've soaked up the history walking the Freedom Trail all afternoon, goes the thinking, there's nothing else to do. In fact, with all those resident students and twenty-somethings to amuse when they've put down the books or left the office, Boston has ample and varied nighttime diversions.

The following are highlights of the social scene, but check the local papers for full listings.

CLUBS

Avalon, 15 Landsdowne Street, tel: 262-2424. With a state of the art light and sound system, infamous Green Room and the Nu Room. Fridays feature the tremendously popular Avaland and nationally known DJs. Sunday is gay night.

The Dance Plex, 262 Friend Street, tel: 720-1966, is a 4 level dance club with 3 dance floors; the music is disco, techno, rave, and 80s new wave.

The Big Easy, 1 Boylston Place, tel: 351-7000, has funk and Motown bands, as well as Top 40 DJs.

Sophia's, 1270 Boylston Street, tel: 351-7001, is a four-story Latin restaurant and nightclub. Live salsa bands, and DJs in the Champagne Lounge. Try the salsa lessons on Tuesdays, Wednesdays or Fridays.

Modern, 36 Landsdowne Street, tel: 351-2581, is a sleek and happening lounge. Elegant glass bar appeals to upscale bar-goers.

COMEDY

Comedy Connection at Faneuil Hall is a regular stand-up venue: 245 Quincy Market, Upper Rotunda, tel: 248-9700.

ImprovBoston is a well known comedy troupe which performs a variety of shows at the Inman Square Theater: 1253 Cambridge Street, Cambridge, tel: 576-1253.

Improvisational **Beantown Madness**, inside Remington's Restaurant, 124 Boylston Street, tel: 482-0110, is a comedy club which offers a wacky experience, including stand-up, magic, juggling, and crazy human tricks.

FILM

Boston Film-Video Foundation, 1126 Boylston Street (tel: 536-1540), highlights work by avant-garde filmmakers. **The Brattle**, 40 Brattle Street, Harvard Square, Cambridge (tel: 876-6837), showing classic, cutting-edge and world films with a different double feature almost every day. **Coolidge Corner Theatre**, 290 Harvard Street, Brookline (tel: 734-2500), a superb 'art film' house in an Art Deco setting.

Harvard Film Archive, 24 Quincy Street, Carpenter Center for the Visual Arts, Harvard University (tel: 495-4700), shows contemporary and classic art films from around the world. **Kendall Square Cinema**, One Kendall Square, Cambridge (tel: 494-9800) and **Nickelodeon Cinemas**, 606 Commonwealth Avenue, Boston (tel: 424-1500), feature off-beat, first-run films, popular with students.

FOLK

Club Passim, 47 Palmer Street, Cambridge (tel: 492-7679), is a journey back to the hippy heyday of Harvard Square. Dinner also served.

Harper's Ferry, 158 Brighton Avenue, Allston, tel: 254-9743. Wide open bar with high ceilings. Features big name R&B acts, local blues artists and bands. Closes at 2am.

JAZZ

Two major venues for top-notch jazz artists compete from opposite sides of the Charles River. **The Regattabar**, Charles Hotel, One Bennett Street, Cambridge (tel: 661-5000), brings greats from McCoy Tyner to local diva Rebecca Parris to Harvard Square. **Scullers**, DoubleTree Guest Suites-Boston/ Cambridge, 400 Soldiers Field Road (tel: 783-0090), has river views and good vibes.

Aficionados seek emerging artists in Inman Square, Cambridge (10 minutes from Harvard Square) at **Ryles**, 212 Hampshire Street (tel: 876-9330). **Wally's Café**, 427 Massachusetts Avenue (tel: 424-1408), is a traditional smoke-filled jazz club.

ROCK/BLUES

Rock supergroups such as Aerosmith and the Cars first won attention in Boston clubs. At **Hard Rock Café**, 131 Clarendon Street (tel: 424-7625), such talismans as a pink-and-black 'Candy-O' jacket, worn by Cars' leader Ric Ocasek, make up the inspirational backdrop for local acts aspiring to follow their lead. Members of Aerosmith recently opened **Mama Kin**, 36 Landsdowne Street (tel: 536-2100), to provide local rockers a nurturing venue. Mama Kin neighbor

Avalon, 15 Landsdowne Street (tel: 262-2424) also hosts new bands.

> **The gay scene**
> Machine, 1256 Boylston Street, tel: 536-1950. Happening nightclub with rotating DJs. Ramrod, 1254 Boylston Street, tel: 266-2986. Especially popular with the leather crowd. Vapor Nightclub and Chaps Lounge, 100 Warrenton Street (Theater District), tel: 695-9500. Large, flashy disco. Also draws a straight crowd. Popular Sunday tea dance from 6–10 pm.

Over the river in Somerville, **Johnny D's**, 17 Holland Street (tel: 776-2004), is the area's most eclectic rock venue. Back in Boston, **The Paradise**, 967 Commonwealth Avenue (tel: 562-8804), is a time-honored home for rock and blues. In Harvard Square, **House of Blues**, 96 Winthrop Street (tel: 491-2583), has a popular Sunday gospel brunch. In Cambridge at Central Square, the **Middle East Restaurant**, 472 Massachusetts Avenue (tel: 492-9181), showcases a wide range of alternative and progressive rock.

When the sun goes down, nightlife begins in this young city

ACTIVITIES

BICYCLING

Those willing to brave the traffic on two wheels can pedal by the Charles River following the **Dr Paul Dudley White Bikeway**. The Bicycle Coalition of Massachusetts, 214A Broadway, Cambridge, MA 02139 (tel: 491-7433) has information and maps.

BILLIARDS

'Pool' is suddenly hip. **Jillian's Billiard Club**, 145 Ipswich St. (tel: 437-0300), and the **Boston Billiard Club**, 126 Brookline Ave. (tel: 536-7665), are popular gathering spots in the Kenmore Square Fenway area.

BIRDWATCHING

One of the country's oldest environmental organizations, the **Massachusetts Audubon Society**, 208 South Great Road, Lincoln, MA 01773 (tel: 781-259-9500), manages several wildlife sanctuaries in the greater Boston area.

JOGGING/ROLLERBLADING

Runners congregate on paths along the Boston and Cambridge banks of the Charles River, as well as on trails through the Emerald Necklace chain of parks. On summer Sundays from 11am to 7pm, Memorial Drive from Eliot Bridge is closed to vehicles. **Beacon Hill Skate Shop**, 135 Charles Street South at Tremont (tel: 482-7400), rents equipment and safety gear.

PARKS

Boston's major green spaces include the sprawling **Arnold Arboretum**, 125 Arborway, Jamaica Plain (tel: 524-1717), home to more than 7,000 kinds of trees and shrubs, and the **Back Bay Fens** (behind the Museum of Fine Arts). Both are part of the **Emerald Necklace** *(see page 55)*.

that runs from the **Public Garden** to **Franklin Park** (for information, contact the city's Parks and Recreation Dept, tel: 635-4505).

For refreshing ocean air, visit **Castle Island Park**, site of Fort Independence, in South Boston, where Edgar Allen Poe served with the army and found inspiration for his tale, *The Cask of Amontillado*. From May to October, take a ferry (no cars) from Long Wharf (Boston Harbor Cruises, tel: 723-7800) to **Boston Harbor Islands State Park** *(see page 91)*.

> **Whale watching**
> A half dozen species of whales inhabit the Stellwagen Bank, a protected maritime sanctuary between Cape Ann and Cape Cod, some 15 miles (24 km) offshore. Trips take 5 hours or more, and run daily from April through September. Operators include New England Aquarium Whale Watch (tel: 973-5281), A.C. Cruise Line (tel: 261-6633), and Boston Harbor Whale Watch (tel: 345-9866). *(See also page 88.)*

SAILING

On the Charles River, between the Hatch Shell and Charles Street pedestrian area, **Community Boating** (tel: 523-1038) has weekly memberships for qualified boaters.

Staff at the **Boston Sailing Center**, 54 Lewis Wharf (tel: 227-4198), take groups of up to six for a two-hour harbor sail.

SKATING

The lagoon at the **Public Garden** is the city's premier skating spot in winter. The town of Brookline also operates a public outdoor rink at **Larz Anderson Park**, 253 Newton Street (tel: 730-2080).

SPECTATOR SPORTS

Baseball: the American League **Boston Red Sox** (tel: 267-1700) play at Fenway Park, the nation's oldest professional diamond, from April to September. Fenway opened in 1912, but its most distinguishing feature – a 37-ft (11-meter) wall behind left field known as the 'Green Monster,' wasn't built until 1934. The park's first season saw the Sox win the World Series – a trick they haven't managed since 1918.

Basketball: the National Basketball Association **Boston Celtics** (tel: 523-3030) play at the new FleetCenter, on Causeway Street beside North Station, from October to May.

Running: first organized in 1897 by the Boston Athletic Association (tel: 236-1652), the **Boston Marathon** is the nation's oldest and attracts the world's finest runners on the third Monday in April (Patriot's Day). 8,000 participants, 1½ million spectators.

Football: on eight Sundays between September and December the **New England Patriots** (tel: 1-800-543-1776) of the National Football League play home games at Foxboro Stadium (25 miles or 40 km from downtown, accessible by commuter rail). Local college teams playing in the city on intermittent Saturday afternoons in the fall include the **Boston College Eagles**, Alumni Stadium, Chestnut Hill (tel: 552-3000); **Boston University Terriers**, Nickerson Field, Brighton (tel: 353-3838); and **Harvard University Crimson**, Harvard Stadium, North Harvard Street, Allston (tel: 495-2211).

Hockey: the **Boston Bruins** (tel: 624-1000) of the National Hockey League skate the FleetCenter ice from October to May.

Rowing: in mid-October, the annual **Head of the Charles Regatta** on the Charles River draws thousands of college teams for the world's largest, single-day crew racing event. Competing boats set off, one after the other, at brief intervals and are timed over the length of the course.

Soccer: Attempts are being made in introduce what Europeans call 'football'. The **New England Revolution** (tel: 508-543-0350; 1-800-543-1776) of Major League Soccer play at Foxboro Stadium, spring and summer.

Tennis: the **US Pro Tennis Championships** are played on the hard courts of the Longwood Cricket Club, 564 Hammond Street, Brookline (tel: 731-2900) in the second week of July.

There are plenty of backwaters to get away from it all

PRACTICAL INFORMATION

Getting There

BY AIR

Logan International Airport, 2 miles (3 km) from downtown in Boston Harbor, has five terminals (A–E). International flights arrive at Terminal E, and there's a free 24-hour inter-terminal shuttle bus. For news of traffic conditions between town and airport, call **Massport's Ground Transportation Hotline** (1-800-235-6426), Mon–Fri, 8am–7pm.

At Airport Station, the MBTA Blue Line connects Logan to downtown in about 10 minutes (fare is 85 cents).

The **Airport Water Shuttle** has daily crossings from Logan to Rowes Wharf (Boston Harbor Hotel) in seven minutes (free shuttle bus operates between ferry dock and all airport terminals); peak period service is every 15 minutes, off-peak is half-hourly, and one-way fare is $10. For cab fare to downtown, expect to pay about $23, including tip and tolls.

BY RAIL

Amtrak's Northeast Corridor passenger service (NYC, Washington DC etc) begins and ends at Boston's South Station (Atlantic Avenue and Summer Street; tel: 482-3660; 1-800-872-7245 or, for hearing-impaired, 1-800-523-6590). South Station is also the eastern terminus for Amtrak's Lake Shore Limited (Chicago etc). All trains stop at Back Bay Station (tel: 722-3200).

BY BUS (COACH)

Boston's sleek bus terminal is at South Station. **Greyhound** (tel:1-800-231-2222), **Peter Pan** (tel: 1-800-343-9999) and **Bonanza** (tel: 720-4110, 1-800-556-3815) have express service to New York City (under five hours) and points in New England. Greyhound and Peter Pan also have terminals at Riverside Station on the MBTA Green Line 'D' branch.

BY CAR

From the west: Route 90 (Mass. Turnpike) has three major city exits — Exits 18-20, Cambridge/Allston (for Cambridge); Exit 22, Prudential Center/Copley Square (for Back Bay); and Exit 24 (for downtown).

From the south: Routes 95, 24 and 3 all feed into Route 128 East, which leads to Route 93 North. Two major exits are Kneeland Street/Chinatown (for Back Bay, Theatre District), and Dock Square (for Airport, North End, Waterfront and Faneuil).

From the north: Routes 1, 93, and 95 enter Boston. Major exits are: Storrow Drive (for Back Bay and Beacon Hill); High Street (for downtown); and Kneeland Street (for Chinatown and Theatre District).

Getting Around

Boston's compact size, good public transportation system, notorious drivers, and confusing streetscape are reasons for hoofing it or hopping on a train. If you must drive, don't expect to find a parking space on the streets, and if you use a garage or car park expect to pay top dollar.

RAPID TRANSIT

Trains: The Massachusetts Bay Transit Authority (MBTA) – known as the 'T' by residents – operates four rapid transit lines (Red, Green, Orange and Blue) that intersect in the downtown area and run between 5am and 1am daily. 'Inbound' means toward downtown; 'outbound' means away from downtown. Green line 'subway' cars (trams) travel on four branches above and below ground: B – Boston College (Commonwealth Avenue, past Boston University); C – Cleveland Circle (Beacon Street via Kenmore Square and Coolidge Corner); D – Riverside (mostly through suburban Brookline and Newton); and E – Heath Street or Arborway (past Museum of Fine Arts, Mass. College of Art, and Northeastern University).

Tokens ($1) are necessary at all underground stations; above ground, tokens or exact change are accepted.

Buses: Route 1 runs along Massachusetts Avenue from Back Bay, across the Charles River, to MIT and Harvard Square. Otherwise, buses are rarely used in the city center. Fare is $0.75 and exact change is required.

Commuter Rail: Trains from **North Station** (Causeway Street beside Fleet Center, on Green and Orange Lines) and **South Station** (Summer Avenue and Atlantic Avenue, on Red Line) serve Concord, Salem, Lowell and Rockport.

Tickets may be bought at stations or on board, subject to a surcharge.

Visitor Pass
The Boston Visitor Pass is valid for unlimited travel on the subway, local buses and inner harbor ferry. One-, three-, and seven-day passes are available and may be purchased on-line from www.mbta.com or by calling 222-5568.

CAR RENTAL
Most big rental companies have locations at Logan Airport and downtown. Alamo, 1-800-327-9633; Avis, 1-800-331-1212; Budget, 1-800-527-0700; Enterprise, 1-800-736-8222; Hertz, 1-800-654-3131; National, 617-661-8747.

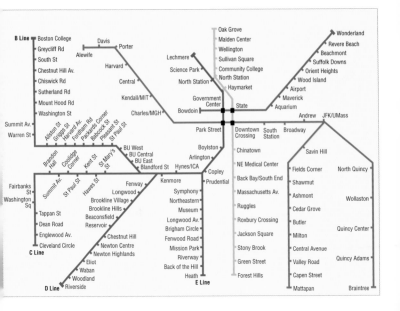

TAXIS

Rather than trying to hail a cab, especially in poor weather, search out a taxi stand outside a hotel: tolls at bridges and tunnels are charged to the rider, but there is no extra charge for more than one passenger. Outside a 12-mile (19-km) radius of downtown, a flat fee is charged.

Facts for the Visitor

TOURIST INFORMATION

Boston Common Visitor Information Center, on Tremont Street (perpendicular to West Street) is a treasure trove of free maps, brochures and information on greater Boston destinations. Open daily 9am–5pm.
National Park Service Visitor Center, 15 State Street (tel: 242-5642), is open daily 9am–5pm.
Greater Boston Convention and Visitors Bureau (tel: 536-4100) provides visitor information Mon–Fri 9am–5pm.

You can also check out the following websites: www.bostonusa.com or www.masstourist.com

FOREIGN CURRENCY EXCHANGE

Convenient brokers include **Thomas Cook Currency Services**, 160 Franklin Street (tel: 1-800-223-9392); **American Express Travel Service,** One Court Street (tel: 723-8400); and numerous **BankBoston** branch offices in Boston and Cambridge (tel: 788-5000). Logan Airport's Terminal E has a convenient exchange counter.

POST OFFICES

The General Mail Facility or main post office is at 25 Dorchester Avenue, behind South Station, and is open 24 hours (tel: 654-5083 for general information). The Post Office at Logan Airport, 139 Harborside Drive, (tel: 567-1090) is also open 24 hours.

OPENING TIMES

Most offices are open Monday to Friday, 9am to 5pm, although some open earlier at 8am.

Shops are generally open daily from 9am to 6 pm, though some open at 10am and stay open later; on Sundays, most stores open at noon.

Banks are open Monday to Friday 9am to 4pm, and often later; Saturday hours are usually 9am to 2pm.

With the exception of Thanksgiving (last Thursday in November), Christmas and New Year's Day, shops, restaurants and other commercial establishments are open seven days a week.

> **Sightseeing tours**
> In this 'walking city,' pedestrian tours by Boston By Foot (tel: 367-2345) are especially popular. Beantown Trolley (tel: 236-2148), and Minuteman Trolley (tel: 876-5539) are actually creatively-fashioned buses that board at hotels and other locations and circulate around major downtown attractions; they'll compete fiercely for your custom. Boston Duck Tours (tel: 723-3825) ride the city's streets in authentic World War II amphibious vehicles, then complete the picture by making a brief waterbound detour into the Charles River.

EMERGENCIES

In Boston and Cambridge, dial 911 (toll-free) for police, ambulance and fire emergencies.

TELEPHONE

The area code for Boston and Cambridge is 617, and the area code for Salem is 978. For directory enquiries, dial 617-555-1212.

WEATHER

For information about the weather service, tel: 936-1234.

VISAS & PASSPORTS

A valid passport is required to enter the United States. Visas are required for some nationalities. Check with your local embassy. Vaccinations are not required.

HEALTH

Health care in the United States is very expensive and foreign visitors are advised to obtain health insurance before leaving home.

MONEY MATTERS

American Express and Visa are the most readily accepted traveler's checks. American Express, Visa, MasterCard and Diners Club credit cards are widely honored, too, but be sure to check with waiters and clerks before you order dinner or have your purchases tallied up.

Be discreet when using credit cards in public; fraudsters may be watching or listening as you use your card during a phone call. To transfer money, call Western Union (tel: 1-800-325-6000).

WHAT TO WEAR

Like most Americans, Bostonians prefer to dress as casually as possible. A very few restaurants and hotels require 'jacket and tie' – the mayor was once refused entrance to the Ritz-Carlton. Some clubs and bars prohibit sneakers and T-shirts.

TIME ZONES

Boston is on Eastern Standard Time (Greenwich Mean Time minus five hours). From the first Sunday in April until the last Sunday in October, the clock is moved forward one hour for Daylight Savings Time. Boston is one hour ahead of Chicago; three hours ahead of Los Angeles; five hours behind London; and 15 hours behind Tokyo.

NEWSPAPERS

Boston's daily papers are the *Globe* (www.boston.com) and *Herald* (www.boston-herald.com); on Thursday, the *Globe*'s pull-out section lists the area's cultural activities, while the Herald's Friday supplement contains listings for the following week. The *Christian Science Monitor* (www.csmonitor.com), a prestigious Boston daily, majors on international rather than local news. The *Boston Phoenix*, an arts and culture weekly, is published on Thursdays. For national and international newspapers and magazines, visit **Out of Town News** (tel: 354-7777) in Harvard Square beside the Red Line 'T' station entrance.

RADIO & TELEVISION

Radio stations in the area include: WBNW on 590AM for business news; WRKO on 680AM for talk; WEEI on 850AM for sports; WCRB on 102.5FM for classical music; WBCN on 104.1FM for rock music; WGBH (Public Radio) on 89.7FM for classical music and jazz; and WBUR (National Public Radio) on 90.9FM for news.

Television stations include Channel 2 (WGBH) for Public Television; Channel 25 (WXNE) for Fox; and Channel 38 (WSBK) for sports. National networks can be viewed on Channel 4 (WBZ) for CBS, Channel 5 (WCVB) for ABC, and Channel 7 (WNEV) for NBC.

Boston with Children

From the swan boats at the Public Garden to the petting zoo at Franklin Park Zoo, Boston abounds with activities of special interest to children.

Museums primarily of interest to adults make an effort to add 'fun' for children. The **Museum of Fine Arts** provides an activity booklet for 'an art adventure' throughout its galleries (children will be mesmerized by the superb collection of Egyptian mummies). The enduring popularity of Robert McCloskey's *Make Way for Ducklings* book, set in the **Public Garden**, makes a stop there a must. In addition to riding the **swan boats** (Apr–Sep 10am–5pm) and feeding the lagoon's resident ducks, small children will want to meet the Mallard family bronze statues at the corner of Charles Street and Beacon Street.

Boston's **Children's Museum**, 300 Congress Street (tel: 426-8855), encourages children to play, dress up, and pretend. Exhibits include a full-scale reconstruction of a Japanese home and climbing apparatus for older kids. Directly beside it, the world's only **Computer Museum** (tel: 426-2800) offers video games, an oversized Walk-Thru Computer, and a gallery of robots and 'smart' machines including, the original R2-D2 from *Star Wars* no less.

> **Airport diversions**
> Energetic young travelers who are waiting for their flights can romp in the Logan Airport Kidport play area located at Terminal C.

The **New England Aquarium**, Central Wharf (tel: 973-5200, *see page 52*) has a Learning Lagoon to give kids the opportunity to touch a variety of artifacts and have their questions answered. The Activity Center is a special place for small children and their families to explore the world of water through a variety of thoughtful activities. To find out more about the Family Activity Center schedule, call 973-6563.

In the Charles Hayden Planetarium at the **Museum of Science**, Science Park (tel: 723-2500), a multi-media 'starship ride' takes specators on a galactic tour and has a child-focused Discovery Center; and the Mugar Omni Theatre with 'wrap-around' screen and sound.

Nearby at the Fleet Center, the **Sports Museum of New England** (tel: 787-7678) lets kids get behind home plate to catch for Red Sox baseball pitching ace Roger Clemens.

At the terminus of the Emerald Necklace, the 72-acre (29-hectare) **Franklin Park Zoo**, one Franklin Park Road (tel: 541-5466), is home to giraffes, gorillas, hippos, leopards, as well as an Australian Outback Trail, and an African tropical forest. There's a butterfly house, Bird's World, and Children's Zoo, too.

ACCOMMODATION

Where to Stay

Metropolitan Boston has well over 20,000 hotel rooms, but booking ahead is recommended, especially in summer and on holiday weekends in the fall. Large conventions can all but lock up the city's major downtown hotels. However, bed and breakfast accommodation is becoming increasingly popular.

Some visitors might prefer the rarefied atmosphere of Cambridge, which is a quick trip (5–10 minutes) from Boston and easily reached by public transport. Another alternative is to stay in one of the many hotels in Greater or Metropolitan Boston and join the MBTA (Massachusetts Bay Transit Authority) commuters for a 30–40 minute journey every morning and evening.

For general information on accommodations, call the Greater Boston Convention and Visitors Bureau toll-free hot line 1-800-888-5515, Monday through Friday, 9am to 5pm.

An approximate guide to current room rates for a standard per night double room is: $$$$ = over $250, $$$ = $200–250, $$ = $100–200, $ = under $100.

Boston
$$$$

Boston Harbor Hotel, 70 Rowes Wharf, tel: 439-7000/1-800-752-7077, fax: 330-9450, www.bhh.com Boston's luxury waterfront hotel – the Airport Water Shuttle to Logan leaves from Rowes Wharf directly outside. All bedrooms have either harbor or skyline views.

Fairmont Copley Plaza Hotel, 138 St. James Avenue, tel: 267-5300/1-800-822-4200, fax: 247-6681, www.fairmont.com Located at Copley Square. Called 'the Grande Dame of Boston' for its opulent Old World architecture.

Four Seasons Hotel, 200 Boylston Street, tel: 338-4400/1-800-332-3442, fax: 423-0154, www.fourseasons.com Overlooking the Public Garden, this is one of the finest hotels in the US. Health club with a lap pool, complimentary downtown limousine, and award-winning restaurant.

Le Meridien, 250 Franklin Street, tel: 451-1900/1-800-543-4300, fax: 423-2844, www.lemeridienboston.com Located in the central Financial District at Post Office Square Park, Boston's newest

There are two staff members to every guest at the original American Ritz

downtown green space; the building (ex-Federal Reserve Bank) was superbly refurbished in the 1980s .

Regal Bostonian Hotel, at Faneuil Hall Marketplace, tel: 523-3600/1-800-343-0922, fax: 523-2454, www.regal-hotels.com Directly opposite Faneuil Hall, the Bostonian is a modern brick structure at the edge of a dense warren of restaurants, grocery shops and butchers.

Ritz-Carlton, 15 Arlington Street, tel: 536-5700/1-800-241-3333, fax: 536-9340, www.ritzcarlton.com A symbol of Boston's graciousness and elegance since 1927, when it was the nation's first Ritz. Two staff members for every guest. Restaurant, lounge and many bedrooms overlook the Public Garden.

Sheraton Boston Hotel & Towers, 39 Dalton Street, tel: 236-2000/1-800-325-3535, fax: 236-1702, www.ittsheratonboston.com With 1,250 rooms, New England's largest hotel. Separate 'Towers' section features butler service. Indoor walking paths connect to Hynes Convention Center, Prudential Center and Copley Place Malls.

Swissôtel Boston, 1 Avenue de Lafayette, tel: 451-2600/1-800-621-9200, fax: 452-0054. www.swissotel.com

Concord's Colonial Inn has more than a hint of the past

European luxury and elegance near Boston Common.

Westin Copley Place, 10 Huntington Avenue, tel: 262-9600, toll-free 1-800-228-3000, fax: 424-7483, www.westin.com Boston's tallest hotel with more than 800 rooms, pool and health club, and three restaurants. Attached to Copley Place and Prudential Center shopping malls.

$$$

Back Bay Hilton Hotel, 40 Dalton Street, tel 236-1100/1-800-874-0663, fax: 867-6158, www.bostonbackbay.hilton.com Boston's only downtown Hilton, near Prudential Center and Christian Science Complex. Boodles restaurant and bar serves over 100 beers from American 'microbreweries.'

Boston Marriot Hotel Copley Place, 110 Huntington Avenue, tel 236-5800/1-800-228-9290, fax: 236-5885, www.marriott.com On edge of Copley Square and Back Bay with indoor pool and health club.

Boston Marriott Hotel Long Wharf, 296 State Street, tel: 227-0800/1-800-228-9290, fax: 227-2867, www.marriott.com Beside New England Aquarium and across from lively Faneuil Hall Marketplace.

Boston Park Plaza Hotel, 64 Arlington Street, tel: 426-2000/1-800-225-

2008, fax: 426-5545. In Back Bay near Public Garden and Theatre District. Exercise and fitness center. Six restaurants, one bar.

Colonnade Hotel, 120 Huntington Avenue, tel; 424-7000/1-800-962-3030, fax: 424-1717, www.colonnadehotel.com Opposite Christian Science Complex and Prudential Center. L-shaped rooms have distinct sitting, sleeping and dressing areas. Seasonal rooftop pool.

Copley Square Hotel, 47 Huntington Avenue, tel: 536-9000/1-800-225-7062, fax: 236-0351, www.copleysquarehotel.com An informal European-style hotel, first opened in the 1890s. Home of the award-winning Café Budapest and the Original Sports Saloon.

Lenox Hotel, 710 Boylston Street, tel: 536-5300/1-800-225-7676, fax: 235-0351, www.lenoxhotel.com Renovated guest rooms, many with working fireplaces. Close to shopping and Copley Place, Prudential Center and Newbury Street. Samuel Adams Brew House at street level.

Omni Parker House, 60 School Street, tel: 227-8600/1-800-843-6664, fax: 227-9607, www.omnihotels.com Where Parker House rolls were created and are still served. Claims to be the oldest continually operating hotel in America, though building dates from 1927. Malcolm X and Ho Chi Minh were once on the staff.

$$

Best Western, 342 Longwood Avenue, Boston, tel: 731-4700; fax: 731-6273, www.bestwestern.com Situated in the heart of the city's medical complex, and close to the Fenway with its colleges and museums. A bus stop at the hotel door means that downtown Boston is only minutes away.

Tremont House Hotel, 275 Tremont Street, tel: 426-1400/1-800-331-9998, fax: 482-6730, www.wyndham.com In the Theater District and close to most attractions. An affordable downtown alternative.

HOSTELS

Berkeley Residence YWCA, 40 Berkeley Street, tel: 375-2524, fax: 375-2525. YWCA-run club has singles and doubles for women only. Also has a restaurant and swimming pool. Located near South Station and Copley Square. $

Boston International Youth Hostel, 12 Hemenway Street, Fenway, tel: 536-9455, fax: 424-6558, www.ymca-boston.com Singles, doubles, quads. Open during summer and early fall for stays of up to 10 days. Access to athletic facilities. Near Symphony Hall, Christian Science Complex, MFA. Green Line of 'T' stops at door, 10 minutes to town. $

YMCA of Greater Boston, 316 Huntington Avenue, Fenway, tel: 536-7800, fax: 267-4653, www.ymcaboston.org Clean rooms with color TV, and full use of athletic facilities. Located near the Prudential Center and Museum of Fine Arts. Downtown is 10 minutes away on Green Line of 'T'.

CAMBRIDGE

Charles Hotel, 1 Bennett Street, tel: 864-1200, fax: 864-5715, www.charleshotel.com Harvard Square's only luxury hotel, overlooking Charles River. Its elegant Rialto restaurant is highly regarded, and the Regattabar considered by many to be the best jazz scene in the region. $$$$

DoubleTree Guest Suites, 400 Soldiers Field Road, tel: 783-0090, 1-800-222-8733, fax: 783-0897, www.doubletreehotels.com An all-suite hotel, located on the Charles River at Storrow Drive (five-minute cab ride to Harvard Square). $$$

Harvard Square Hotel, 110 Mount Auburn Street, tel: 864-5200, fax:

864-2409. A six-story hotel located in the heart of Harvard Square. All rooms have picture windows. Complimentary continental breakfast. **$$**

The Inn at Harvard, 1201 Massachusetts Avenue, tel: 491-2222, 1-800-528-0444, fax: 520-3711, www.innatharvard.com At the gates of Harvard University, with sunlit atrium dining room. Some rooms have tiny balconies. **$$$**

Sheraton Commander, 16 Garden Street, tel: 547-4800, 1-800-325-3535, fax: 868-8322, www.sheratoncommander.com Near Harvard and Radcliffe. Some rooms have kitchenettes. Restaurant and café. **$$–$$$**

INNS, GUEST HOUSES, B&Bs

A room for two usually costs between $85 and $185. In Boston, many guest houses and B&Bs are situated along Newbury Street,

82 Chandler Street, 82 Chandler Street, South End, tel: 482-3450. A 56-room inn located in the center of the city. Private baths, direct dial telephones, and color televisions. **$–$$**

Beacon Inn Guest Houses, 248 Newbury Street, tel: 266-7142. Kitchenette or refrigerator is provided in each room. Close to Fenway Park. **$–$$**

Carolyn's B&B, 102 Holworthy Street, Cambridge, tel: 864-7042. Small, cozy B&B with cheerful rooms; private or semi-private baths. **$–$$**

Eliot and Pickett Houses, 25 Beacon Street, tel: 248-8707. Two brick townhouses on Beacon Hill with a total of 20 guest rooms. **$–$$**

Newbury Guest House, 216 Newbury Street, tel: 437-7666. On Back Bay's busiest street for shopping and dining. **$–$$**

BED & BREAKFAST AGENCIES

Bed & Breakfast Agency of Boston, 47 Commercial Wharf, tel: 720-3540, fax: 523-5761, www.boston-bnbagency.com Downtown's largest selection of historic B&B homes, including Federal and Victorian townhouses, yachts, and beautifully restored 1840s waterfront lofts.

Host Homes of Boston, PO Box 117, Waban Branch, tel: 244-1308. A moored yacht in the harbor and a Victorian townhouse in the Back Bay are just some of the unusual listings.

Bed & Breakfast Associates Bay Colony, tel: 720-0522, 1-800-347-5088, www.bnbboston.com Lists homes in metropolitan Boston and throughout the eastern part of Massachusetts.

CONCORD

Colonial Inn, 48 Monument Square, tel: 978-369-9200. Originally built in 1716, and operating as a hotel since 1889; with 56 rooms, and a good restaurant. **$$–$$$**

GLOUCESTER

Cape Ann Motor Inn, 33 Rockport Road, tel: 978-281-2900. On Long Beach, with balconies and kitchenettes. **$–$$**

Vista Motel, 22 Thatcher Road, tel: 978-281-3401. Overlooking Good Harbor Beach; some rooms with balconies; kitchenettes. **$–$$**

ROCKPORT

Addison Choate Inn, 49 Broadway, Tel: 978-546-7543. Walk to town center; classic Yankee styling. **$–$$**

The Tuck Inn, 17 High Street, tel: 978-546-7260. A 1790 colonial home near the station and a short walk from the village center. **$$**

SALEM

Hawthorne Hotel, On the Common, tel: 508-744-4080, 1-800-729-7829. Furnished with 18th-century reproductions, within walking distance of waterfront, museums, historic sites and shopping areas. **$$**

INDEX